GENESIS *of a* LEGACY

LEADER'S GUIDE

BASED ON THE WRITINGS AND VIDEO PRESENTATIONS OF

KEN HAM & STEVE HAM

COMPILED BY STACIA MCKEEVER

TABLE OF CONTENTS

Genesis *of a* Legacy

Introduction

Answer Key

Resources   139

Index   141

GENESIS *of a* LEGACY

The Psalmist, guided by the Holy Spirit, wrote in Psalm 127:3–5 (NASB):

> Behold, children are a gift of the LORD,
> The fruit of the womb is a reward.
>
> Like arrows in the hand of a warrior,
> So are the children of one's youth.
>
> How blessed is the man whose quiver is full of them;
> They will not be ashamed
> When they speak with their enemies in the gate.

Truly, children are a blessing and gift from the Lord and a source of great joy to parents. Yet children can also be the cause of great heartache to many parents. We see disobedient children throwing temper tantrums in the supermarket. Schools are filled with wild and unruly students. Increasingly, even children of Christian parents are "leaving the fold" once they graduate and head off on their own.

While each individual child is responsible for his decisions and behavior before the Lord, the Bible is full of commands to parents regarding how they should train up their children and warnings of what will happen if they do not fulfill the instructions of the Creator. With this curriculum, our desire is not to merely provide "how-to" instructions on child-rearing, but rather to exhort parents to understand that raising their children is their *ministry*, not merely another job on their list of things to do. Parents who instill in their families a love for the Lord are, in effect, carrying out the Great Commission given to us by our Lord and Savior (Matthew 28:19–20). Truly, raising godly children is one of the means by which our Creator enables us to fulfill this command.

The Lord has promised to give us everything we need for life and godliness through our knowledge of Him who called us to eternal life (2 Peter 1:3). Although each child is unique and individual circumstances vary greatly, God has promised that His

Word is profitable for teaching, reproof, correction and training in righteousness so that the man of God may be thoroughly equipped for every good work (2 Timothy 3:16–17).

Throughout this course we'll be discussing what the Bible—the Word of the One who created us and called us to eternal life—teaches about raising children to be godly. We'll be addressing questions such as the following:

+ What is my goal in raising my children?

+ How can I make the Bible "real" to my children?

+ What does the Bible say about my role in my family?

+ What does the Bible say about discipline?

+ How do I know God's Word is an all-sufficient parenting guide?

+ How can I effectively communicate the truths of Scripture to my children?

+ What are my educational choices?

+ What should I teach my children about being wise stewards of their possessions?

Over the next 11 weeks, Ken Ham (president and CEO of *Answers in Genesis*) and his younger brother Stephen Ham will be our guides as we discover that the genesis of the legacy we leave for our children begins as we love the Lord and accept His Word as our authority, committing to use it to guide us in all areas of our lives.

How to Use This Curriculum

Session Requirements

For each lesson, you will need:

+ DVD player, projector, screen (if not using your computer to play the DVDs)

+ Leader's Guide

+ Bible

+ The appropriate number of copies of participants' worksheets (one set per person—permission is granted to copy the worksheets from the accompanying DVDs or download them from www.AnswersInGenesis.org/go/GOAL). We suggest purchasing (or having each participant purchase) a 3-hole ring binder for each participant to keep their worksheets in (a printable "cover sheet" for the binder is available on the accompanying DVD).

NOTE: Participants may elect to purchase a copy of this manual for themselves, instead of using the worksheets. Additional copies of this guide are available from AnswersBookstore.com or by calling 1-800-778-3390.

Participant's Requirements

For each lesson, the participant will need:

+ Participant worksheets (which feature the lesson outline, discussion questions, homework and list of suggested resources)

+ Bible

+ Writing tool

Lesson Components

We provide a lesson overview and lesson objectives for the leader at the beginning of each lesson.

Each lesson should take approximately 60 minutes to complete and is divided into the following components:

1. Getting Started (12 minutes)

   During this time, welcome the participants to the session, make any announcements, begin with prayer, etc.

   Spend five minutes reviewing the homework from the previous week. Encourage participants to share what they've learned and to hold each other accountable for what they're learning.

   Go over the "Getting Started" section with participants. Answers for these questions can be found in the Answer Key.

2. Lesson (25–35 minutes)

   This course is a combination of video-led and facilitator-led sessions. Six sessions (1, 2, 3, 8, 9, 11) feature videos by either Ken Ham or Steve Ham, while the other five sessions (4, 5, 6, 7, 10) are to be led by the facilitator. Please go over the lessons during the previous week, asking your pastor or church leaders any questions that you may have concerning the content of the lesson. We have provided room in the margins for any notes you wish to make.

   Illustrations and *Putting It into Practice* segments for the facilitator-led sessions can be found on the corresponding DVD. The *Putting It into Practice* video segments (found on the accompanying DVDs) featured throughout the lesson and the discussion time are meant to be an encouragement to participants and to provide practical ideas on how to implement many of the concepts addressed in the sessions. For these segments, we interviewed godly parents from Bible-believing churches who have raised—or are in the process of raising—their children to follow the Lord. Encourage participants to jot down any ideas that might be helpful to them as they watch these short (3–4 minute) segments.

3. Bringing It Home (13–23 minutes)

    The questions provided in this section are designed to help participants to evaluate what they heard in the lesson and think about how they can apply it to their lives. You may want to break your class into smaller groups to discuss the questions.

    Answers for these questions can be found in the Answer Key.

    End the session with prayer that the Holy Spirit would enable participants to apply the truths they have learned.

4. Frequently Asked Questions

    In many lessons, we offer short answers to some of the more frequently asked questions concerning parenting and the Bible and point them toward resources which address the questions in more detail. You may want to go over these during class or assign them as homework.

5. Homework

    This section is designed to encourage participants to continue to evaluate and apply the content of the lesson during the following week.

6. For More Information

    There are many excellent resources that can encourage believers in their walk with the Lord and in their desire to parent their children. These are featured in these sections and, unless otherwise noted, are available from AnswersBookstore.com or by calling 1-800-778-3390. A complete list of all resources is provided on pages 139–140.

How to Get the Most out of This Curriculum

1. Be flexible as you facilitate the group discussion. We have provided suggested responses; however, allow participants to discuss their views, within reason, while guiding them to understand what the Bible teaches.

2. Take your time as you go through the questions—feel free to spend more time on some questions over others. Allow the participants' interest level to guide the discussion.

3. Do not allow any one person to monopolize the discussion—be careful to include all participants.

4. If participants aren't able to finish all the "Bringing It Home" discussion questions during the allotted time, suggest they take some time during the week to answer them.

About the *Genesis of a Legacy* Curriculum and Book

The *Genesis of a Legacy* curriculum is based on the DVDs featuring Ken Ham and Steve Ham. Their same-titled book (not included with the curriculum, but available at AnswersBookstore.com) adds an historical perspective to this topic as they address in more detail the legacy their father left them and their siblings.

Acknowledgments

We would like to thank the following people for their help in writing and editing this course:

Dave Mateer, father of 3 (Family Heritage Bible Chapel)
Rhonda Musser, mother of 4 (Bible Chapel of Delhi Hills)
Steve Wilt, father of 3 (Kenton Baptist)

We also wish to thank the following individuals for their participation in the *Putting It into Practice* segments.

Parental mission statements

Pastor Brad Bigney, father of 5 (Grace Fellowship)
Tony Ramsek, father of 3 (Heritage Family Bible Chapel)
Dave and Ellen Liebing, parents of 5 (Bible Chapel of Delhi Hills)
Steve Fazekas, father of 4 (Grace Fellowship)
Ron Uebel, father of 2 (Heritage Family Bible Chapel)
Jim Stiles, father of 1 (Smyrna Missionary Baptist)
H.A. and Rhonda Musser, parents of 4 (Bible Chapel of Delhi Hills)

Using evolutionary propaganda

Mark Looy, father of 3 (Grace Fellowship)
Carl Kerby, father of 2 (Big Bone Baptist)

Educational philosophy

Pastor Brad Bigney, father of 5 (Grace Fellowship)
Charmaine Shazier, mother of 3 (First Baptist of Walton)

Ron Uebel, father of 2 (Heritage Family Bible Chapel)
Kim Hoffman, father of 2 (Washington Baptist)
Dave and Ellen Liebing, parents of 5 (Bible Chapel of Delhi Hills)

Homeschool and socialization

Pastor Brad Bigney, father of 5 (Grace Fellowship)
H.A. and Rhonda Musser, parents of 4 (Bible Chapel of Delhi Hills)

Scripture memory

Dave and Ellen Liebing, parents of 5 (Bible Chapel of Delhi Hills)
Dale and Karen Mason, parents of 4 (Grace Fellowship)
Pastor Cecil and Vicki Eggert, parents of 3 (Calvary Baptist)
Ron Uebel, father of 2 (Heritage Family Bible Chapel)
H.A. and Rhonda Musser, parents of 4 (Bible Chapel of Delhi Hills)
Charmaine Shazier, mother of 3 (First Baptist of Walton)
Tony Ramsek, father of 3 (Heritage Family Bible Chapel)

Non-leading husbands

Dave and Ellen Liebing, parents of 5 (Bible Chapel of Delhi Hills)
H.A. and Rhonda Musser, parents of 4 (Bible Chapel of Delhi Hills)

Sacrificial love

Steve Wilt, father of 3 (Kenton Baptist)
Steve Fazekas, father of 4 (Grace Fellowship)
H.A. and Rhonda Musser, parents of 4 (Bible Chapel of Delhi Hills)
Pastor Brad Bigney, father of 5 (Grace Fellowship)
Pastor Cecil and Vicki Eggert, parents of 3 (Calvary Baptist)

Child-centered homes

Pastor Brad Bigney, father of 5 (Grace Fellowship)
Dave and Ellen Liebing, parents of 5 (Bible Chapel of Delhi Hills)
Tony Ramsek, father of 3 (Heritage Family Bible Chapel)
Ron Uebel, father of 2 (Heritage Family Bible Chapel)

Family devotions

Gary and Missy Vaterlaus, parents of 3 (Community Fellowship)
Pastor Brad Bigney, father of 5 (Grace Fellowship)
Ron Uebel, father of 2 (Heritage Family Bible Chapel)
Tony Ramsek, father of 3 (Heritage Family Bible Chapel)
Steve Fazekas, father of 4 (Grace Fellowship)
Lindsey Eggert (Calvary Baptist)

Pastor Cecil and Vicki Eggert, parents of 3 (Calvary Baptist)

Finding a spouse

April Mason (Grace Fellowship)
Dale and Karen Mason, parents of 4 (Grace Fellowship)
Steve Wilt, father of 3 (Kenton Baptist)
H.A. and Rhonda Musser, parents of 4 (Bible Chapel of Delhi Hills)
Dave and Ellen Liebing, parents of 5 (Bible Chapel of Delhi Hills)
Gary and Missy Vaterlaus, parents of 3 (Community Fellowship)
Ron Uebel, father of 2 (Heritage Family Bible Chapel)

Parental transparency

Dave and Ellen Liebing, parents of 5 (Bible Chapel of Delhi Hills)
Pastor Brad Bigney, father of 5 (Grace Fellowship)
Luke Eggert (Calvary Baptist)
Frost Smith, mother of 1 (Bible Chapel of Delhi Hills)
Pastor Cecil and Vicki Eggert, parents of 3 (Calvary Baptist)
H.A. and Rhonda Musser, parents of 4 (Bible Chapel of Delhi Hills)

Biblical discipline vs. abuse

Ron Uebel, father of 2 (Heritage Family Bible Chapel)
Tony and Christy Ramsek, parents of 3 (Heritage Family Bible Chapel)
Pastor Brad Bigney, father of 5 (Grace Fellowship)
Dave and Ellen Liebing, parents of 5 (Bible Chapel of Delhi Hills)

Why won't my children listen?

H.A. Musser, father of 4 (Bible Chapel of Delhi Hills)
Pastor Brad Bigney, father of 5 (Grace Fellowship)
Ron Uebel, father of 2 (Heritage Family Bible Chapel)
Tony and Christy Ramsek, parents of 3 (Heritage Family Bible Chapel)
Dave and Ellen Liebing, parents of 5 (Bible Chapel of Delhi Hills)

Deuteronomy 6 principle

Steve Wilt, father of 3 (Kenton Baptist)
Tony Ramsek, father of 3 (Heritage Family Bible Chapel)
Vicki Eggert, mother of 3 (Calvary Baptist)
Pastor Cecil and Vicki Eggert, parents of 3 (Calvary Baptist)

Santa Claus and your children

Dave and Ellen Liebing, parents of 5 (Bible Chapel of Delhi Hills)
Charmaine Shazier, mother of 3 (First Baptist of Walton)

Kim Hoffman, father of 2 (Washington Baptist)
Ron Uebel, father of 2 (Heritage Family Bible Chapel)

Missions and your children

Carl Kerby, father of 2 (Big Bone Baptist)
Luke and Lindsey Eggert (Calvary Baptist)
Rhonda Musser, mother of 4 (Bible Chapel of Delhi Hills)
Ron Uebel, father of 2 (Heritage Family Bible Chapel)

Children and finances

Sam Dingus, father of 4 (Erlanger Baptist)
Dale and Karen Mason, parents of 4 (Grace Fellowship)
H.A. and Rhonda Musser, parents of 4 (Bible Chapel of Delhi Hills)
Pastor Brad Bigney, father of 5 (Grace Fellowship)

Provoking children

H.A. Musser, father of 4 (Bible Chapel of Delhi Hills)
Dave and Ellen Liebing, parents of 5 (Bible Chapel of Delhi Hills)
Ron Uebel, father of 2 (Heritage Family Bible Chapel)
Steve Fazekas, father of 4 (Grace Fellowship)

Media monitoring

Dale and Karen Mason, parents of 4 (Grace Fellowship)
Tony Ramsek, father of 3 (Heritage Family Bible Chapel)
Ron Uebel, father of 2 (Heritage Family Bible Chapel)
Gary and Missy Vaterlaus, parents of 3 (Community Fellowship Church)
Pastor Brad Bigney, father of 5 (Grace Fellowship)
Sam Dingus, father of 4 (Erlanger Baptist)
Rhonda Musser, mother of 4 (Bible Chapel of Delhi Hills)
Dave and Ellen Liebing, parents of 5 (Bible Chapel of Delhi Hills)

SESSION 1

THE GENESIS FAMILY

You will need DVD 1 for this lesson

Overview

Money, property, an original Van Gogh, a set of old baseball cards, an antique china cabinet. These are the types of items usually mentioned when parents discuss the legacy they will leave for their children. Yet all of these are only temporal. In this lesson, Ken Ham challenges parents (and parents-to-be) to consider the legacy they will leave for their children—is it an inheritance of things temporal or of things eternal?

With a brief tour of history, Ken discusses the legacy left by three men—John Bunyan, Martin Luther and Charles Darwin—and the lasting impact their legacies have had, not just on their children, but on the world. On a more personal note, Ken explains the inheritance he gained from his father: a heart for reaching people with the gospel and a love for the Word of God.

He ends with the challenging question: What inheritance are you leaving for your children, friends and neighbors?

Objectives

At the end of this lesson, participants should be able to:

+ Explain what the greatest legacy is that a parent could leave for his child.

+ List the courses of action one should take when encountering an idea that seems to contradict biblical teachings.

+ Begin drafting a mission statement for parenting.

Getting Started

 Welcome participants to class, open in prayer, make announcements, etc.

The Creator has promised to give us everything we need for life and godliness through our knowledge of Him who called us to eternal life (2 Peter 1:3). Although each child is unique, and individual circumstances vary greatly, God has promised that His Word is profitable for teaching, reproof, correction and training in righteousness so that the man of God may be thoroughly equipped for every good work (2 Timothy 3:16–17). Throughout this course we'll be discussing what the Bible—the Word of the One who created us and called us to eternal life—teaches about how to leave a godly legacy for our children.

Before we watch the video, let's talk for a moment about how we would answer the following questions.

1. The title of this course is *The Genesis of a Legacy*. What do you think of when you hear the word "legacy"?

2. What type of legacy or inheritance did your parents leave for you?

3. Briefly describe the legacy you are trying to leave for your children.

4. Briefly describe the goals you have set for your children.

The Genesis Family video outline

 Play *The Genesis Family* DVD.

Proverbs 13:22

> A good man leaves an inheritance for his children's children. (NIV)

Isaiah 38:19

> The father to the children shall make known thy truth. (KJV)

Ephesians 6:4

> And, ye fathers, provoke not your children to wrath: but bring them up in the nurture and admonition of the Lord. (KJV)

Deuteronomy 6:6–7

> These commandments that I give you today are to be upon your hearts. Impress them on your children. Talk about them when you sit at home and when you walk along the road, when you lie down and when you get up. (NIV)

One inheritance a parent can leave for his children: A love for the Word of God

Philippians 3:7–8

> But whatever was to my profit I now consider loss for the sake of Christ. What is more, I consider everything a loss compared to the surpassing greatness of knowing Christ Jesus my Lord, for whose sake I have lost all things. I consider them rubbish, that I may gain Christ. (NIV)

The most important inheritance a parent can leave for his children: A spiritual inheritance

The legacy of John Bunyan (1628–1688)

> *Pilgrim's Progress*
>
> Tomb in Bunhill Fields
>
> Memorials in Bedford

The legacy of Martin Luther (1483–1546)

> The Reformation
>
> Statue and memorials in Worms: *Here I stand, I can do no other, God help me.*

The legacy of Charles Darwin (1809–1882)

> *On the Origin of Species*
>
> Popularized "molecules-to-man" evolutionary processes
>
> Memorials in Shrewsbury
>
> There is no absolute truth
>
> Evil fruits of unbiblical thinking (racism, abortion, homosexual behavior)
>
> "Biological arguments for racism may have been common before 1850, but they increased by orders of magnitude following the acceptance of evolutionary

theory." *Ontogeny and Phylogeny*, Stephen Jay Gould, Belknap-Harvard Press, 1977, p. 127–128.

"How special are human genes? Some of us think that we humans have a special place in the animal kingdom. However, the human genome is similar to a chimpanzee's, and has a lot in common with the genome of a fruit fly." Sign at the London Natural History museum

The legacy of Mervyn Ham (1928–1995)

Love for the Word of God

Gave a defense for his faith

1 Peter 3:15

But in your hearts set apart Christ as Lord. Always be prepared to give an answer to everyone who asks you to give the reason for the hope that you have. But do this with gentleness and respect, (NIV)

What to do when something contradicts what the Bible teaches:

Make sure I'm reading the passage correctly

Wait for answers—only God knows everything

Teach your children *how* to think, not just *what* to think

Challenge: What inheritance are you leaving for your children, friends and neighbors?

Bringing It Home

 Use this time to discuss the following questions with participants. Many of the illustrations used in the video are available on the DVD for you to refer to as necessary.

1. King Herod wanted to be known as a great builder. He built a massive, luxurious palace at Caesarea Philippi, and he constructed three luxurious palaces on the top of the famous mountain known as Masada. As far as we know from history, Herod's spiritual state was such that he died without receiving the Lord, and thus he faced eternal separation from God—suffering the "second death." His soul lives on forever, but the great buildings he had constructed as his legacy on Earth have all but crumbled into dust. Herod was not concerned about his soul or the soul of anyone else, including those of his children—he was more concerned about the material things of this world (that don't last).

    Read Matthew 6:19–24. Although the Bible doesn't prohibit possessing material goods or leaving a monetary inheritance for our children, it warns against placing more importance on temporary possessions than on the eternal. In what areas are you focusing more on leaving your children an earthly inheritance rather than a heavenly inheritance?

In what ways can you begin to "store up for yourselves treasure in heaven"?

2. Although Martin Luther, John Bunyan, Jonathan Edwards and Charles Spurgeon left behind many volumes for their children and others to read, the inheritance they left for their children didn't stop there. They also took care to instill in their children a personal, spiritual heritage, continually pointing their children toward the Savior. How do the spiritual heritages of these men compare to the legacy you are leaving for your children?

3. Read Deuteronomy 10:12 and Matthew 22:34–40. What goal does God set forth in these verses for us and our children?

In light of these verses, let's return to a question we asked at the opening of this session: "Briefly describe the legacy you are trying to leave for your children." Does the legacy you are trying to leave for your children line up with the legacy the Creator wants you to leave?

Watch *Putting it into practice—Parenting mission statements.*

4. If you were asked to describe in a sentence or two your mission statement for raising your children, what would it be?

5. We often hear news stories about findings that seem to contradict what the Bible plainly teaches. List some of the accounts that you've heard recently.

How can we respond when we hear such news items?

 Close in prayer, and briefly go over the homework assignment with participants.

Homework

1. The book of Proverbs contains a wealth of information on training children. Over the next few weeks, we'll be reading through the entire book of Proverbs. For this week, read Proverbs 1–5 with your spouse (we suggest reading one chapter per day). In a journal, write down the insights that both of you glean from these chapters. Additionally, consider the following questions:

   + What do these proverbs teach about discipline?

   + What does Solomon teach about the nature of children in these verses?

   + How did Solomon communicate with his children in this passage?

   + Solomon frequently compares the behavior of the wise to the behavior of the foolish. What are the characteristics of the wise? Which behaviors characterize the life of the foolish? Make a list of the characteristics of each. Is your life more characteristic of the wise or of the foolish? Because we can do nothing apart from the Lord, ask Him to show you areas in which you need to put off foolish behavior and put on the behavior of the wise. As you pray, ask Him to help you train your children to be wise. Most importantly, pray with an attitude of belief (read James 1:5–6).

2. This course assumes that the Bible is the Word of God and, as such, is the ultimate authority in all areas it touches on. If your children were to ask you "How do you know the Bible is God's Word?" how would you reply? If you are having trouble formulating a response, spend some time this week researching the answer. See www.AnswersInGenesis.org/go/bible and www.AnswersInGenesis.org/go/existence for help.

3. If you aren't familiar with the writings or lives of Martin Luther, John Bunyan, Jonathan Edwards or Charles Spurgeon take some time to learn more about them and the legacy they left behind. (See the For More Information section for suggested resources.)

4. Prayerfully begin working on developing a mission statement with your spouse that will provide direction to you as you seek to raise children who love and honor the Lord. What does the Creator want for your children? What verses can you use to guide you? This activity can continue over the next 10 weeks.

For More Information

+ *Luther* (book or DVD)

   Born of humble parents in Eisleben, Germany, in 1493, Martin Luther grew up to live an adventuresome, often dangerous life as a man of God. His life taught many lessons to others, and his thoughts and words and actions have helped to make our modern world what it is. This insightful biographical book contains full-color pictures from the well-documented 2003 movie.

+ *Pilgrim's Progress* (curriculum)

   This large-format book contains the entire original text of *The Pilgrim's Progress* with John Bunyan's own Scripture annotations, plus a special photo-illustrated section about the man who penned this classic while in jail. Within its illustrated pages are "Truths to Ponder" for young children and "Digging Deeper" questions for older students and adults. It also includes activity ideas, character studies and commentary regarding the unique figures that Christian encounters during his journey to the Celestial City.

+ *The Forgotten Spurgeon* by Iain Murray

   This book traces the main lines of Spurgeon's spiritual thought in connection with the three great controversies in his ministry.

- *Spurgeon: The Early Years*, Banner of Truth Trust

  This biography covers the time period from Spurgeon's birth in 1834 through his call to the ministry in 1851 as a boy preacher, to the laying of the foundation of Metropolitan Tabernacle in 1859.

- *Spurgeon: The Full Harvest*, Banner of Truth Trust

  This sequel deals with Spurgeon's later preaching, sermonic activities, literary labors and other related events from the Down Grade Controversy to his death in 1892.

- *Marriage to a Difficult Man: The Uncommon Union of Jonathan and Sarah Edwards* by Elizabeth Dodds

  This biography gives a wonderful peek at the home life of America's most eminent theologian, highlighting his loving relationship to his wife and 11 children.

- *Jonathan Edwards: A New Biography* by Iain Murray

  Iain Murray's meticulous research and careful, yet warm, writing style does justice to the private and public life of Jonathan Edwards. This book is the definitive work on the life of this great theologian.

- *John Bunyan: His Life, Times, and Work* by John Brown

  This is the standard biography on the famous writer of *Pilgrim's Progress*. Available from Amazon.com.

- www.AnswersInGenesis.org/go/bible

- www.AnswersInGenesis.org/go/existence

THE GENESIS OF A WORLDVIEW

You will need DVD 1 for this lesson

Overview

During this session we'll explore in more detail the legacy that Mervyn Ham left in the form of the message that his son preaches to the world. Mervyn Ham's hunger for knowing and upholding the Word of God instilled in Ken Ham a desire to do the same. In seeking to answer the questions the world was using to attack the Bible, Ken developed a message in which he shows how the Bible's history is linked to the Bible's message of salvation. When the historical aspects of the Bible's narrative are undermined, ultimately the basis for the gospel is destroyed. This message is called the "Relevance Message."

In this lesson, Ken provides a brief overview of this relevance message and, in the process, challenges parents to evaluate their own worldview—is it truly biblical? He addresses questions that deal with death and suffering, fossil formation, natural selection and information theory. He stresses the importance of teaching our children how the Bible connects to the world—showing them that the Bible is true when it touches on areas dealing with things we see and hear, and thus the message of salvation is also true.

He reiterates the importance of parents training their children in the nurture and admonition of the Lord and ends with the story of the Aborigines, an example of a culture in which the fathers forgot to teach their children about the Lord. The challenge is: What can we, as parents, do to ensure that we don't forget to tell our children about the Creator?

Objectives

At the end of this lesson, participants will be able to:

+ Provide an answer to the question "How can there be a loving God in this world full of death and suffering?"

+ Explain how the Bible's history relates to its morality and the implications this has for parenting.

+ Explain the two-pronged approach to restoring biblical authority in our families and culture.

Getting Started

 Welcome participants to class, open in prayer, make announcements, etc.

In the last session, we were challenged to consider the legacy we are leaving for our children. In this session, we'll explore how Ken's father, Mervyn Ham, has impacted thousands because of the heritage he passed on to his children. We'll learn the importance of teaching our children how the Bible connects to our everyday lives, and how we can be prepared to answer the questions our children ask us. But first, let's consider the following questions.

1. In the recent past, the world has experienced terrible devastation in the form of tsunamis, earthquakes, hurricanes, terrorist attacks and the spread of deadly diseases. When such tragedies unfold, the inevitable question that arises is "How can there be a loving God in the midst of all this death and suffering?" If you were asked this question, how would you respond?

2. As the Word of God, the Bible must be our authority in every area of our life—including how to raise children. However, many people reject biblical authority because of questions they have concerning fossils, rocks, change in animals and the like. What questions have caused *you* to question some of the teachings of the Bible? Or what questions have you heard from others who question the teachings of the Bible?

The Genesis of a Worldview video outline

 Play *The Genesis of a Worldview* DVD.

Isaiah 38:19

> The father to the children shall make known thy truth. (KJV)

The outcome of a father making known the truth to his children: The Relevance Message

Matthew 19:4–6

> And he answered and said unto them, Have ye not read, that he which made them at the beginning made them male and female, And said, For this cause shall a man leave father and mother, and shall cleave to his wife: and they twain shall be one flesh? Wherefore they are no more twain, but one flesh. What therefore God hath joined together, let not man put asunder. (KJV)

The Bible's history-doctrine connection

Because the history is true, the doctrine is true

The foundation (directly or indirectly) of all biblical doctrines is in Genesis 1–11

> First coming
>
> Origin of sin
>
> Last Adam
>
> New heavens and Earth
>
> Clothing
>
> Origin of death
>
> Seven-day week

Creation's original state

Genesis 1:29–30

> Then God said, "I give you every seed-bearing plant on the face of the whole earth and every tree that has fruit with seed in it. They will be yours for food. And to all the beasts of the earth and all the birds of the air and all the creatures that move on the ground—everything that has the breath of life in it—I give every green plant for food." And it was so. (NIV)

Genesis 9:3

> Everything that lives and moves will be food for you. Just as I gave you the green plants, I now give you everything. (NIV)

Death was not present but is the penalty for sin

Reconciling a loving God with a world full of death and suffering

We rebelled against God, in Adam

We told God, "We want life without you"

God is gracious and merciful and He sent a Savior

The fossil record: evidence of death, disease and suffering

Darwin's legacy: Death has always been a part of the creation

Preparing to give a defense for the faith

Grand Canyon formation

Fossil formation

Stalactite / stalagmite formation

Opal formation

Change in animals

Origin of genetic information

The source of absolute truth

The philosophy of evolutionary and "millions of years" ideas

The problem

Attack on authority of God's Word (Genesis 1–11 in this era of history)

The solution

Restore foundation of authority of Word of God

Battle foundationally secular humanism

The Aborigine example

Joshua's reminder

Joshua 4:21–22

> He said to the Israelites, "In the future when your descendants ask their fathers, 'What do these stones mean?' tell them, 'Israel crossed the Jordan on dry ground.' (NIV)

Judges 2:7–8

> The people served the LORD throughout the lifetime of Joshua and of the elders who outlived him and who had seen all the great things the LORD had done for Israel. Joshua son of Nun, the servant of the LORD, died at the age of a hundred and ten. (NIV)

Judges 2:10–11

> After that whole generation had been gathered to their fathers, another generation grew up, who knew neither the LORD nor what he had done for Israel. Then the Israelites did evil in the eyes of the LORD and served the Baals. (NIV)

Challenge: How can we ensure that we don't forget to tell our children?

Bringing It Home

 Use this time to discuss the following questions with participants. Many of the illustrations used in the video are available on the DVD for you to refer to as necessary.

1. Read Romans 5:12. Ultimately, who should receive the blame for the presence of death and suffering in the world?

2. Every breath that we take should remind us of God's grace and mercy. Why?

3. While out walking one day, you and your son stumble across the remains of a bird that was attacked by a cat. Your son turns to you and asks, "Daddy, why did that cat attack and kill this poor bird?" How do you respond?

4. Ken explained that one of the main problems in Western society today is that evolutionary and/or "millions of years" ideas have undermined the Bible's teaching in many areas. He offered a defensive and an offensive tactic for restoring biblical authority.

   In what ways can we *defensively* battle the attack on God's Word?

   In what ways can we take the *offense* in this battle?

5. What is the connection between accepting Genesis 1–11 as true historical narrative and accepting what the Bible teaches about raising children?

6. One afternoon, you take your family to a museum of natural history and you come across a sign that reads: "Paleontologists believe that birds like this cassowary are living descendants of dinosaurs. Dinosaurs evolved as a specialized branch of the reptile family tree. Birds are a continuation of this branch, and thus, are dinosaurs themselves." Or, say, you're watching a nice family movie with your children in which one of the characters says, "Dinosaurs evolved into birds over millions of years." How would you handle situations such as these?

 Watch *Putting It into Practice—Using evolutionary propaganda*.

 Close in prayer, and briefly go over the homework assignment with participants.

Homework

1. During this week, read Proverbs 6–10 with your spouse (we suggest reading one chapter per day). In your journal, continue writing down the insights that both of you glean from these chapters. Additionally, consider the following questions:

   + What do these proverbs teach about discipline?

   + What does Solomon teach about the nature of children in these verses?

   + How does Solomon communicate with his children in these passages?

   + Solomon frequently compares the behavior of the wise to the behavior of the foolish. What are the characteristics of the wise? What behaviors characterize the life of the foolish? Make a list of the characteristics of each as you go through this book. Is your life more characteristic of the wise or of the foolish? Because we can do nothing apart from the Lord, ask Him to show you areas in which you need to put off foolish behavior and put on the behavior of the wise. As you pray, ask Him to help you train your children to be wise. Most importantly, pray with an attitude of belief (read James 1:5–6).

2. What challenges to the Bible have you heard that were not addressed in this lesson? Perhaps you've asked yourself the questions listed below. Take some time this week to explore the answers to these questions. Visit the "Get Answers" page at www.AnswersInGenesis.org/go/qa for assistance.

   + Who was Cain's wife?

   + Isn't the observable process of natural selection the same as evolution?

   + Haven't many transitional forms been found that prove evolution has happened in the past?

   + Aren't there methods of dating the earth that reveal it to be many millions of years old?

   + What about carbon dating?

   + Where did the different people groups come from?

   + Couldn't God have used evolutionary processes to create?

   + Does it really matter how old the earth is?

   + Haven't bacteria been shown to evolve?

3. Continue working on drafting a family mission statement that will help you and your spouse to parent your children. What does the Creator want for your children? What verses can you use to guide you?

For More Information

   + *War of the Worldviews* edited by Gary Vaterlaus

   How are we to respond when we hear of the latest "argument" for evolution? How can we prepare our children to face the evolutionary indoctrination of our public schools and universities? What are we to make of "Christian" organizations that teach the big bang and millions of years? How can we build a truly biblical worldview?

   In this book, you will find ammunition for the war: answers to some of the most common arguments for evolution, analyses of Christian compromise and a call for a return to true biblical authority.

- *The Revised and Expanded Answers Book* edited by Don Batten

  This essential book addresses the most common questions that both Christians and non-Christians ask regarding creation/evolution and Genesis. It answers twenty of the most-asked questions, such as: "Cain's wife—who was she?" and "What about continental drift?"

- *Always Ready* by Greg Bahnsen

  This compilation of Dr. Greg Bahnsen's published works on Christian apologetics includes his apologetics syllabus and articles on common apologetic questions. Practical "weapons" for every Christian's spiritual arsenal.

- *The 7 C's of History* (*Answers in Genesis*)

  This curriculum explains to children the foundational events of biblical history in seven fun lessons: Creation, Corruption (the Fall of man), Catastrophe (Noah's Flood), Confusion (the Tower of Babel), Christ, Cross and Consummation (the new heavens and new Earth). Great for homeschool, Sunday school, Christian school or family devotions.

- *Beginnings* (*Answers in Genesis*)

  This curriculum enables children to answer foundational questions of the Christian faith, such as: Where did God come from? How did we get the Bible? How old is the earth? Did God create in six actual days? What about the "dating" methods? What is compromise? Great for homeschool, Sunday school, Christian school or family devotions.

- *Answers Academy* (*Answers in Genesis*)

  The purpose of the Answers Academy apologetics curriculum is to equip viewers to answer the questions the world is asking about the authority and accuracy of the Bible. During the thirteen illustrated lessons, your class or small group will discover why it is vital to provide logical answers to skeptics, and how to give those answers with a solid understanding of what the Bible says about geology and astronomy.

- www.AnswersInGenesis.org/go/curse

- www.AnswersInGenesis.org/go/qa

- www.AnswersInGenesis.org/go/bird-evolution

SESSION 3

VEGEMITE KIDS

You will need DVD 2 for this lesson

Overview

Education is a hot topic today. Should we send our children to public school? Should we give them a Christian education at a Christian school? Should we educate our children at home? Although there are many factors to consider when choosing an educational path for your children, parents should primarily base their decision on what the Bible teaches about this area.

In this third and final video with Ken, he shares that the family has been ordained by God to transmit knowledge of Himself from one generation to the next. Ken underscores that the Bible clearly teaches that the father is to be responsible for leading and seeing that his family is taught about the knowledge of God and what He has done for us. He offers many insights concerning the biblical command to be the "salt of the earth" and challenges parents to rethink their educational philosophy. He provides some cautions about public schools and Christian schools that have compromised on God's Word. He exhorts parents to raise "Vegemite Kids" by developing in their children a love for God and His Word.

Ken emphasizes that raising children is an incredible responsibility—a responsibility that should not be taken lightly. He ends with the challenge he gave in the first video, "What legacy are you leaving your children?"

Objectives

At the end of this lesson, participants should be able to:

+ Explain the biblical principles to consider when developing a philosophy of education.

+ Devise a Scripture memory plan to implement with their family (or commit to continue one already in place).

+ Articulate the incredible responsibility that parents have in raising children.

Getting Started

 Welcome participants to class, open in prayer, make announcements, etc.

We saw in the last lesson that developing a truly biblical worldview and teaching this to our children is of vital importance. In this lesson, we'll be challenged to consider *how* we're educating our children and what the Bible teaches about this foundational area.

1. Let's discuss for a few minutes your philosophy of education. How have you decided that your children will be educated? Why did you choose that path? What biblical principles guided your decision?

Vegemite Kids video outline

 Play *Vegemite Kids* DVD.

A function of the family

Malachi 2:15

Has not the LORD made them one? In flesh and spirit they are his. And why one? Because he was seeking godly offspring. So guard yourself in your spirit, and do not break faith with the wife of your youth. (NIV)

Transmit the knowledge of God from one generation to the next

The father as the spiritual leader

Isaiah 38:19

The father to the children shall make known thy truth. (KJV)

Ephesians 6:4

And, ye fathers, provoke not your children to wrath: but bring them up in the nurture and admonition of the Lord. (KJV)

Psalm 78:3–8, 11

What we have heard and known, what our fathers have told us. We will not hide them from their children; we will tell the next generation the praiseworthy deeds of the LORD, his power, and the wonders he has done. He decreed statutes for Jacob and established the law in Israel, which he commanded our forefathers to teach their children, so the next generation would know them, even the children yet to be born, and they in turn would tell their children. Then they would put their trust in God and would not forget his deeds but would keep his commands. They would not be like their forefathers—a stubborn and rebellious generation, whose hearts were not loyal to God, whose spirits were not faithful to him. They forgot what he had done, the wonders he had shown them. (NIV)

Educational considerations

Matthew 5:13

You are the salt of the earth (NIV)

Mark 9:50

Have salt in yourselves (NIV)

2 Timothy 3:14–15

But as for you, continue in what you have learned and have become convinced of, because you know those from whom you learned it, And how from infancy [a child] you have known the holy Scriptures, which are able to make you wise for salvation through faith in Christ Jesus. (NIV)

Psalm 51:5

Surely I was sinful at birth, sinful from the time my mother conceived me. (NIV)

1 Corinthians 15:33

Do not be misled: "Bad company corrupts good character." (NIV)

Ephesians 4:14

That we henceforth be no more children, tossed to and fro, and carried about with every wind of doctrine, by the sleight of men, and cunning craftiness, whereby they lie in wait to deceive; (KJV)

1 Corinthians 13:11

> When I was a child, I talked like a child, I thought like a child, I reasoned like a child. When I became a man, I put childish ways behind me. (NIV)

Build Christianity from foundation up, rather than impose it top down

Teach what to believe and why we believe it

Public school considerations

The myth of neutrality

Matthew 5:13

> You are the salt of the earth. But if the salt loses its saltiness, how can it be made salty again? It is no longer good for anything, except to be thrown out and trampled by men. (NIV)

Mark 9:50

> Salt is good, but if it loses its saltiness, how can you make it salty again? Have salt in yourselves, and be at peace with each other. (NIV)

"When asked to estimate the likelihood that they will continue to participate in church life once they are living on their own, levels dip precipitously to only about one of every three teens." Barna Research Online, Teenagers Embrace Religion but Are Not Excited About Christianity, www.barna.org, January 10, 2000.

Please note that the "88% of the children raised in evangelical homes leave church at the age of 18" statistic Ken references was later found to be based on unreliable research. However, the following statistic provides another example of the same trend:

"...whereas 52% of the students report frequent attendance at religious services during the year prior to entering college, only 29% report frequent attendance during their junior year (an absolute drop of 23%)." Preliminary Findings on Spiritual Development and the College Experience: A Longitudinal Analysis (2000-2003). www.spirituality.ucla.edu/results/Longitudinal_00-03.pdf

"A minority of born again adults (44%) and an even smaller proportion of born again teenagers (9%) are certain of the existence of absolute moral truth." Barna Research Online, The Year's Most Intriguing Findings, www.barna.org, December 12, 2000.

Revelation 3:16

> So because you are lukewarm, and neither hot nor cold, I will spit you out of My mouth. (NASB)

College considerations

Jeremiah 10:2

This is what the LORD says: "Do not learn the ways of the nations [the heathen] or be terrified by signs in the sky, though the nations are terrified by them." (NIV)

How much is the world influencing your children? How much are you influencing your children?

Philippians 3:7–8

But whatever was to my profit I now consider loss for the sake of Christ. What is more, I consider everything a loss compared to the surpassing greatness of knowing Christ Jesus my Lord, for whose sake I have lost all things. I consider them rubbish, that I may gain Christ. (NIV)

Jeremiah 9:23–24

This is what the LORD says: "Let not the wise man boast of his wisdom or the strong man boast of his strength or the rich man boast of his riches, but let him who boasts boast about this: that he understands and knows me, that I am the LORD, who exercises kindness, justice and righteousness on earth, for in these I delight," declares the LORD. (NIV)

Eternal considerations

"Wherefore, see to it, that you cause your children first to be instructed in spiritual things, that you point them first to God, and, after that, to the world. But in these days, this order, sad to say, is inverted. In my judgement there is no other outward offense that in the sight of God so heavily burdens the world, and deserves such heavy chastisement, as the neglect to educate children." Martin Luther treatise, Letter to the Majors and Alderman of all the cities of Germany in behalf of Christian schools.

"I would advise no one to send his child where the Holy Scriptures are not supreme. Every institution that does not unceasingly pursue the study of God's word becomes corrupt. Because of this we can see what kind of people they become in the universities and what they are like now. The universities only ought to turn out men who are experts in the Holy Scriptures, men who can become bishops and priests, and stand in the front line against heretics, the devil, and all the world. But where do you find that? I greatly fear that the universities, unless they teach the Holy Scriptures diligently and impress them on the young students, are wide gates to hell." Martin Luther, *To the Christian Nobility of the German Nation Concerning the Reform of the Christian Estate*, 1520, trans. Charles M. Jacobs, Rev. James Atkinson, The Christian in Society, I (Luther's Works, ed. James Atkinson, vol. 44), 1966, p. 207.

"I am convinced that the battle for humankind's future must be waged and won in the public school classroom by teachers who correctly perceive their role as the proselytizers of a new faith: a religion of humanity that recognizes and respects the spark of what theologians call divinity in every human being. These teachers must embody the same selfless dedication as the most rabid fundamentalist preachers, for they will be ministers of another sort, utilizing a classroom instead of a pulpit to convey humanist values in whatever subject they teach, regardless of the educational level—preschool day care or large state university. The classroom must and will become an arena of conflict between the old and the new—the rotting corpse of Christianity, together with all its adjacent evils and misery, and the new faith of humanism." John Dunphy, A Religion for a New Age, *Humanist*, Jan.–Feb. 1983, p. 26.

Challenge: What legacy are you leaving your children?

Bringing It Home

 Use this time to discuss the following questions with participants. Many of the illustrations used in the video are available on the DVD for you to refer to as necessary.

1. We discovered in a previous lesson that our primary goal in raising our children should be to develop in them a love for God and His Word, guiding them toward maturity in Christ. Although individual circumstances vary greatly, each of us is responsible before God for the education of our children. Up to this point, what have your educational decisions for your children been based on? What are your educational goals for your children?

    As you consider your educational options, think about the following:

    +   How much time do you need to spend "reprogramming" your children after a day at school?

    +   Are the people that you've chosen to educate your children helping or hindering you in developing godly attitudes in your children?

    +   Is the educational situation in which you've placed your children such that it will help them develop a Bible-based view of the world?

    +   Are your children's teachers actively involved in training your children, or are they turning them away from things of the Lord?

    +   How can you become more involved in your children's educational process so that you can help to offset the ungodly attitudes and actions they are being taught?

♦   Is the educational choice that you've made for your children for God's glory, or have you made it out of a sense of pride, because of an "antiestablishment" philosophy or because of a desire for academic superiority?

 Watch *Putting It into Practice—Educational philosophy* for varied perspectives on educating children.

2. Read 2 Timothy 3:15–16; Deuteronomy 11:18–21; Joshua 1:7–8; Colossians 3:16 and Psalm 119:11. According to these passages, why is it important to know and memorize Scripture?

How are you currently helping your children to memorize Scripture? In what ways can you teach your children to know the holy Scriptures from infancy? If your children are able to talk, develop a plan for helping them to begin memorizing Scripture, if you haven't already.

 For some ideas on ways to help children memorize Scripture, watch *Putting It into Practice—Scripture memory*.

Of course, it is important that we, as parents, are actively committing the words of God to our memory, as well. Are you doing this?

3. Read John 3:36 and John 5:24. What do John the Baptist and Jesus teach about the eternal nature of our children (and our friends and neighbors)?

Although every individual is responsible before God for the decision he makes regarding the gift of eternal life, the Bible is clear that we also have a responsibility to tell our children about their need for God's grace and mercy. Read Romans 10:11–15 and Ephesians 6:4. We'll develop this thought further in later lessons.

Frequently Asked Question

1. Should we be concerned that if we homeschool our children they may not develop socially?

   One concern that some parents express when considering educational options is the "socialization" factor. They are concerned that their children learn to interact with others appropriately in social situations. What do the following passages have to say about this topic? Proverbs 22:24-25; Jeremiah 10:2 and 1 Corinthians 15:33

 View the *Putting It into Practice—Homeschool and Socialization* session for some ways that homeschooling parents respond to this concern.

 Close in prayer, and briefly go over the homework assignment with participants.

Homework

1. During this week, read Proverbs 11–15 with your spouse (we suggest reading one chapter per day). In a journal, write down the insights that both of you glean from these chapters. Additionally, consider the following questions:

   + What do these proverbs teach about discipline?

   + What does Solomon teach about the nature of children in these verses?

   + How does Solomon communicate with his children in this passage?

   + Solomon frequently compares the behavior of the wise to the behavior of the foolish. What are the characteristics of the wise? What behaviors characterize the life of the foolish? Make a list of the characteristics of each as you go through this book. Is your life more characteristic of the wise or of the foolish? Because we can do nothing apart from the Lord, ask Him to show you areas in which you need to put off foolish behavior and put on the behavior of the wise. As you pray, ask Him to help you train your children to be wise, also.

2. Read Psalm 78:8–72. What does Asaph say happened to the Israelites when fathers failed to teach their children about the Creator and what He had done for them?

3. Spend some time this week talking to your spouse about your current educational situation. Are both of you happy with it? Are there ways you can change it so

that your children are learning to view the world from a biblical perspective? Are there ways that both of you can become more involved in the educational process, making sure that your children are developing a love for God and His Word and growing in Christ-likeness? Ask the Lord for wisdom as you consider your educational options.

4. Read Psalm 119:1–88. Write down ten principles that you have gleaned from what David teaches about the Word of God.

5. Continue working on drafting a family mission statement that will help you and your spouse to parent your children. What does the Creator want for your children? What verses can you use to guide you?

For More Information

+ A great way to learn more about homeschooling is to visit TheHomeschoolMagazine.com.

+ The Christian Law Association provides guidelines for the rights that Christians have in public schools at www.christianlaw.org/defending_schools_pf.html.

+ *A Christian Philosophy of Education* by Dr. Gordon Clark

This book teaches readers how to develop a true Christian philosophy of education based upon the Bible. The author also helps parents understand that there is no such thing as neutrality in education and that the real nature of the public education system is an anti-Christian agenda.

+ For those considering sending their children to college, visit www.AnswersInGenesis.org/go/cec for suggestions about which college to attend and a questionnaire to send to colleges that helps to ascertain the college's views on certain issues.

SESSION 4

GOD-GIVEN ROLES IN MARRIAGE

You will need DVD 2 for this lesson

Overview

During the past three sessions, Ken Ham has repeatedly emphasized the role that husbands and fathers are to have in their families. In this session, we will take the time to look at what the Bible teaches about the father's role as a husband in more detail. In addition, we'll be examining what the Bible teaches about the role of the wife. We will also develop the biblical basis for marriage, God's ordained purposes for marriage and how the Fall has affected the marital relationship.

Preparing for the Lesson

This is the first lesson in which the teaching section is led by you, the facilitator, rather than by video. Please spend time going over the material in this lesson during the week before you are scheduled to present this lesson.

+ The illustrations and *Putting It into Practice* segments are available on DVD 2.

+ If you, as the instructor, have any appropriate personal anecdotes that enhance or illustrate the points made in this lesson and honor the Lord, please feel free to add them as you go along.

+ We have provided multiple Bible passages to read and study throughout these facilitator-led sessions. The verses in parentheses are supplemental to the primary verses and may be read as you have time (otherwise, encourage participants to read them during the following week).

♦ For the sake of time, you may want to write the passage references given throughout the lesson on individual slips of paper beforehand and pass them out to participants, asking them to read their assigned passage at the appropriate time. Or you may want to have everyone turn to the passage being discussed. The decision is left to you.

Objectives

At the end of the lesson, participants should be able to:

♦ Explain the origin of marriage.

♦ Explain the God-ordained purposes of marriage.

♦ Explain the corruption of marriage found in the history in Genesis.

♦ Explain the roles of husband and wife in relationship to one another.

Getting Started

 Welcome participants to class, open in prayer, make announcements, etc.

Ken Ham asked this question in a previous session, but let's return to it for a moment. In many Christian homes, who is it that leads the family spiritually? Do you agree or disagree with his statement? Why or why not?

Lesson

ILLUSTRATION 4-00

Although Ken has repeatedly stressed the father's role in leading his family in his previous session, during this lesson we'll be exploring what this means in more detail, as well as looking at the wife's role. The primary reason we need to practice these principles is obedience to our Creator, and thus to glorify and please Him (2 Corinthians 5:9). Secondarily, following the Creator's commands will allow us to have a home that runs efficiently and will give our children a sense of security knowing that their parents love each other and work together for God's purposes. Prayerfully, they will grow up observing godly marriage principles they can reproduce in their own marriages, should the Lord call them to such a covenant.

Let's begin by looking at some of the basics of the marriage relationship: where it came from, why it was established and what has happened to it.

A. Basics of marriage

1. The origin of marriage

ILLUSTRATION 4-01

 Read Genesis 1:24–31 and Genesis 2:4–25[1] (Matthew 19:4–6)

From these passages, we can see marriage is *not* just another social institution that has gradually evolved over the millennia into what it is now. The marriage relationship was established at the very beginning of creation. In fact, Jesus affirmed this truth when He was speaking with the Pharisees about divorce (Matthew 19).

The marriage of a man and woman is blessed by the Creator (Genesis 1:28), and elsewhere we read that he who finds a wife finds what is good and obtains favor from the Lord (Proverbs 18:22).

2. Some purposes of marriage

a. Companionship

ILLUSTRATION 4-02

God determined that it was not good for the man to be alone and that man needed a suitable helper to help him do the work the Lord had given him to do (Genesis 2:15). Notice in this passage that Adam did *not* find a suitable helper from within the animal kingdom. And instead of creating another being from the dust of the ground, God used the man He had created in His image to create the man's helper—*woman,* which in Hebrew literally means "she-man" or "man-ess." The idea of the wife being a companion in marriage is also mentioned in Proverbs 2:17 and Malachi 2:14 (albeit in a negative context).

b. Be fruitful and multiply

ILLUSTRATION 4-03

Another reason God ordained the institution of marriage is to provide a way for a man and woman to be fruitful and multiply (Genesis 1:28). This principle is touched on again in Malachi 2:15. God desires for us to have children that will honor Him.

---

[1] For a refutation of the oft-repeated canard that Genesis 1 and 2 are contradictory accounts of Creation, see www.AnswersInGenesis.org/go/genesis-contradictions.

3. **Corruption of marriage**

    ILLUSTRATION 4-04

     Read Genesis 3

    The original relationship between the man and his wife was a perfect one. However, the entire universe was affected by Adam and Eve's disobedience to the commands of God (Romans 8:20–22). This sin changed the fellowship we have with God and each other.

    Adam and Eve were no longer the perfect beings God had originally created. Although they retained the image of God, that image was corrupted by the sin now in their lives. As the federal head of the human race, Adam made a choice which also affected his descendants (Romans 5:12). Each of us, as a child of Adam, is a sinner—this includes the beautiful little babies that we bring into the world. Let's take a few minutes to remind ourselves of our true nature.

    ILLUSTRATION 4-05

     Read Psalm 51:1–6, Romans 3:9–18 and 1 John 1:8

    What do these passages teach us about us and our children?

    > Answer: Allow participants to discuss that these verses show that we are not born "inherently good," but are all born sinners in rebellion against God. This applies to everyone—young and old, male and female. We are deceiving ourselves if we think that we do not have to contend with a sin nature in ourselves, our spouse or our children.

    Specific to our topic of marriage, our sinful nature drives us to prideful, selfish behavior that harms our spouse and perverts the roles God has assigned to husbands and wives. We'll take a look at some of those roles next.

B. **Roles in marriage**

    (This section highlights some of the primary roles God has assigned to husbands and wives in their marriage relationship. Many excellent Christian books are devoted strictly to the topic of what the Bible says about husband and wife roles; we are unable to be so comprehensive here. Additional Scripture verses and resources are included in the "Homework" and "For More Information" sections, respectively.)

1. **Equal, but different roles**

   ILLUSTRATION 4-06

    Read 1 Peter 3:7 and Galatians 3:28

   In a very important sense, husbands and wives are equal. Men and women are equally powerless to free themselves from their slavery to sin, the blood of Christ being the necessary and sufficient atonement before a holy God to cover them both. Thus, in Christ, husbands and wives are fellow heirs of the grace of life, one in Christ Jesus.

   Equality, however, does not preclude distinction in roles.

    Read Philippians 2:5-8 (Matthew 26:36-39; John 4:27-34; John 6:35-40)

   In this passage, what attitude is Jesus (equal with God) displaying toward the Father?

   > Answer: Allow participants to discuss that Jesus says that He is here to do the will of the Father. He took on the form of a servant—humble and willing to put others first. Although He expressed His own desire (Matthew 26:39), He willingly laid aside what He wanted in order to do the will of His Father. He was completely submissive to the Father's will.

    Read 1 Corinthians 11:3 (Ephesians 5:22-24; 1 Timothy 2:11-12)

   What is the God-prescribed authority structure for husbands and wives?

   > Answer: The husband is to be the head of the wife. Recognize, however, that husbands are not the ultimate authority. They, too, are to be under the authority of Christ.

2. **For both: Love God; love one another**

   ILLUSTRATION 4-07

    Read Matthew 22:35-40

   Every specific instruction that we will discuss (and in the "Homework" section) is a subset of the greatest commands (which apply to both husbands and wives) to love God with every part of your being, and to love your neighbor as yourself.[2] Your closest neighbor, of course, is your spouse. God-first and others-next living is the prescription against our normal (in the flesh) selfishness.

   In the home, this means a continually increasing pattern of devotion to God and service to each other. The following principles (granted, these are simplistic) might help:

---

[2]   The modern abuse of this verse that sees a third command (to love yourself) in the "two commandments" is vigorously rejected. This error comes from psychology-influenced eisegesis (see session 8). A more thorough treatment can be found in Jay Adams, *The Biblical View of Self-Esteem, Self-Love & Self-Image* (Eugene, OR, Harvest House Publishers, 1986).

◆ For those decisions involving situations addressed directly or indirectly in Scripture, you and your spouse should stand firm together, searching and being obedient to God's Word.

◆ For those decisions involving preferences (for example, where to stop to eat during a long car trip), you should "argue" for what would most please your spouse.

3. **For husbands: sacrificially love your wife**

ILLUSTRATION 4-08

 Read Ephesians 5:22–33

In this passage, Paul teaches that the marriage relationship is to be a picture of the relationship between Christ and the church. Specifically, husbands are commanded to love their wives in the same way that Christ loved the church.

How does Christ love the church? How does this apply to your relationship with your wife?

Allow participants to contemplate this analogy. Some relationships include:

· Christ gave Himself for the church; husbands are to sacrifice for their wives.

· Christ sanctifies the church; husbands should desire to see their wives sanctified and encourage them thus.

· Christ nourishes and cherishes the church; husbands are to nourish (physically and spiritually) and cherish their wives.

 Watch *Putting It into Practice: Sacrificial love*.

4. **For wives: submit to your husband**

ILLUSTRATION 4-09

 Read Genesis 2:18–24 and Ephesians 5:22–33 (Colossians 3:18; Titus 2:5; 1 Peter 3:1–6)

Eve was created as a helper for Adam, and this same honorable role is to be fulfilled by wives today. The husband has responsibility for setting and maintaining the direction of the family. Thus, the wife's role is to submit to her husband's authority, obediently and diligently implementing and enforcing his instructions, helping him accomplish the tasks he has set forth, showing him the utmost respect.

What is the church's relationship to Christ? How do those principles apply to your relationship with your husband?

Answer: Allow participants to contemplate this analogy. Some relationships include:

· The church exists to serve Christ; the woman's role as wife is to serve her husband.

· The church receives her instruction from Christ; wives receive their direction from their husbands (this does not preclude their personal communion with Christ, of course).

Of all the commands that God gives to wives, the "submission" command is perhaps the one most rejected. And yet, we've seen that even Jesus Christ—the Creator God—was Himself willingly submissive to the will of the Father. Men and women alike bear the image of God (Genesis 1:27) and are sinners equally in need of His saving grace (Galatians 3:28). The Creator chose to create man first and to designate him to be the leader in the home, for His glory. To women, He gave the privilege of being a helper to their husbands and bearing children, for His glory.

When we attempt to reverse God's lovingly prescribed order, we disobey the commands of God, just as our first parents did in the garden. We also set a poor example for our children to follow. If we want to raise children who will be obedient to the commands of God, then we ourselves need to model obedience to the Creator.

Bringing It Home

1. Let's return to the question we asked at the beginning of this session. Does it really matter which parent is leading the family?

2. What are some ways you can serve and "argue for" the desires of your spouse?

3. Husbands, what are some ways you can fulfill your role as head of your family?

Frequently Asked Questions

1. Can a husband remain the leader of his family and delegate some responsibility to his wife or others?

    Along with the idea of biblical headship comes the idea of responsible delegation. As he oversees and manages his household, a father may choose to delegate some responsibilities to his wife or children. For most home-schooling families, for example, it will be the wife who is at home during the best times for formal instruction. The husband certainly can assign the wife the task of overseeing this instruction. This does not mean he is hands-off; he is still responsible for keeping abreast of how things are going, what is being taught, etc.

2. My husband is totally uninterested in leading our family. What do I do?

    In some cases, a wife may desire for her husband to lead his family, but the husband is unwilling to do so. Her primary responsibility is to pray for her husband and continue to maintain a submissive and respectful attitude toward her beloved.

 Watch *Putting It into Practice: Non-leading husbands* for some ideas on how a wife can handle such situations.

3. How does my relationship with my spouse change when we have children?

    Children are welcome additions to our families and are a blessing from the Lord, but our nurturing and admonition of them should complement, not compete with, the relationship we have with our spouse. Of course, raising our children will take precedence at times because children require a lot of time and energy. But the work in which you labor together should serve to bond you closer to your spouse, not drive you away from one another.

    After the individual's relationship with the Lord, the husband-wife relationship is clearly to be the primary relationship within the family. Too often, we allow our homes to become centered on our children and we forget to continue developing the husband-wife relationship. Your children will someday leave you, but you have made a covenant before the Lord to stay married to your spouse for as long as you live.

    Think about some practical ways you can demonstrate to your children that your relationship with your spouse takes priority. Some examples might include giving her priority in time, priority during a discussion and taking her on dates.

4. I never had any good role models of being a godly husband and have no idea how to lead my home. What should I do?

    Find some godly men in your local body of Christ to spend time with. Humbly ask them to teach you how to lead your family according to biblical principles. Try to establish a regular meeting time with them to study the Bible and discuss any problems that you may be facing. As always, search the Scriptures to see if the things they are teaching you line up with biblical principles.

5. Since Eve was created from Adam's rib, does this mean that men have one less rib than women?

    Not at all. Even though Adam may have lost his rib, the genetic information that coded for the rib was still present in his body, and thus was passed on to his descendants. For example, imagine that a man loses his finger in a car accident. Would this mean that any children born to him after the accident would have one less finger as well? Of course not. Additionally, ribs can grow back! See www.AnswersInGenesis.org/go/rib.

 Close in prayer, and briefly go over the homework assignment with participants.

Homework

Before going through the homework passages, let us offer a word of encouragement and exhortation. These passages set a standard of which we all fall short. We need to remember that God is gracious to us in our shortcomings and that we need to be continually seeking Him and the grace and mercy that He offers to His children.

A. For husbands

1. The following passages reveal specific instructions and standards God has given to men. As you read these passages, make a list of the characteristics that are ascribed to men of God.[3] Choose five of the passages to memorize and meditate on. Ask the Lord to help you as you seek to grow to be more like His Son.

Genesis 2:24	1 Corinthians 7:2–5, 11	1 Thessalonians 2:11–12
Deuteronomy 6:1–9	1 Corinthians 14:35	1 Timothy 3:2–9
Psalm 78:1–7	Ephesians 5:23–32	Titus 1:6–9
Proverbs 13:22, 24	Ephesians 6:4	Titus 2:1–2
Isaiah 38:19	Colossians 3:19, 21	1 Peter 3:7

2. This week, talk to your wife about your role as a leader in your home. Humbly ask her for three specific areas in which she thinks you could better fulfill your role as husband … father … companion … leader.

---

3   We'll also be looking at the qualifications given for elders and deacons. Even though a husband may not hold an office in the church, he is still called to exhibit characteristics given for these men in his home—these are the standards to which God holds *all* men.

3. Take some time this week to evaluate how you view your wife. Do you have a truly biblical perspective on this gift from the Lord, or is she merely your maid, your dishwasher, your <fill in the blank>? Read Solomon's words to his beloved in Song of Solomon. How did Solomon treat her? How did he talk about her?

4. In what ways have you fallen short of loving your wife and children sacrificially? What desires and wants do you have that you are putting before the needs and wants of your family?

5. As the head of the home, your life is to reflect that of Christ's. After this course is completed, spend some time learning more about your example as you study the life of Christ by reading the first four books of the New Testament. What did Jesus teach and how did He act? More specifically, read Matthew 5–7. In what areas do you need to grow and become more submissive to Christ's authority and the other authorities He has placed in your life?

B. For wives

1. As you read through the following verses that describe for us the various responsibilities God has given to wives and mothers, make a list of the characteristics of a godly woman. Choose five of the passages to memorize and meditate on. Ask the Lord to help you as you seek to conform to the image of His Son.

Genesis 2:18	Proverbs 23:13–14	1 Timothy 2:9–15
Proverbs 1:8	Proverbs 31	1 Timothy 3:11
Proverbs 6:20	1 Corinthians 7:2–5, 10	1 Timothy 5:9–10, 14
Proverbs 12:4	Ephesians 5:22, 33	Titus 2:3–6
Proverbs 19:13	Colossians 3:18	1 Peter 3:1–6

2. Humbly ask your husband for three specific areas in which he thinks you could better fulfill your role as wife … mother … companion … helper.

3. In a Bible dictionary, look up the word "respect." What does it mean?

4. Take some time to evaluate your attitude toward your husband. Do you have an attitude of submission and respect, as the Bible commands, or does your attitude run counter to what the Bible teaches? Do you really believe that helping your husband is to be your primary ministry on Earth? What other good ministry opportunities or responsibilities tend to "compete with" your primary ministry of being helpmate to your husband?

C. For husbands and wives

1. One of the aspects discussed in Genesis 2:24 of a God-honoring marriage is that of leaving father and mother in order to start a new family. Have both of you truly abandoned your dependence on your parents and committed to cleaving only to your spouse?

2. Many Christian couples read 1 Corinthians 13 during their wedding ceremony. Read it again and make a list of the characteristics of love given in this passage to remind yourselves of the loving standard God has given us. Notice that the descriptions of love that Paul gives are all *actions*. Love is not merely a feeling that comes and goes with the circumstances, but it is a commitment which is acted out in many ways. Which aspects of loving according to God's standard do you need to work on, with His help?

3. Pray together and ask the Lord to help each one of you to fulfill the roles and responsibilities that He has given you. Pray *for* each other daily, as well.

For More Information

*   *The Exemplary Husband* by Stuart Scott

    God ordained marriage between a man and a woman for companionship, pro-creation, and so man would have a suitable helper. However, God says much more in the Bible about husbands loving their wives than He says about wives submitting to their husbands. He created marriage to be a picture of the relation-ship between Christ and the church. Christ was willing to sacrifice His life for the church, and God expects no less from husbands today. The overall purpose of this book is to assist husbands toward purposeful and lasting Christlikeness for the glory of God.

*   *The Complete Husband* by Lou Priolo

    What does it take to be a "biblical husband"? Written in an easy-to-understand style, Priolo's guide attempts to teach husbands how to love their wives as Christ loves the church. The solid biblical teaching explores the how-to of loving your spouse, provides a crash course on communication skills, offers advice on sexual relations and more.

+ *The Excellent Wife* by Martha Peace

  Who is an excellent wife? What is she like? Using the woman in Proverbs 31 as a model, trusted Christian counselor Peace offers detailed practical answers to questions most often asked by Christian wives. Her proven principles and scripturally based insights will encourage you to become the wife God wants you to be. This is a must-read for every Christian wife.

+ *Christian Living in the Home* by Jay Adams

  This book is full of practical, biblical advice on Christ-centered family living, communicating with family members, family guidance and discipline, living with an unbelieving spouse and many other areas.

+ *Love Life for Every Married Couple* by Ed Wheat

  This classic is possibly the best book available about marriage issues, including romantic love and sexuality as God intended it! Great for Christian couples who recognize God's Word as the absolute authority.

God-Given Roles in the Family

You will need DVD 3 for this lesson

Overview

In the previous lesson, we looked in detail at the origin, purpose and corruption of the family relationship. We also examined the biblically prescribed roles for husbands and wives. In this session, we'll take a detailed look at the role the Bible calls children to fill. We'll see the necessity for children to submit to their parents' authority in the Lord. We'll also take a brief look at the dangers of allowing our children to run the household.

Preparing for the Lesson

This is the second lesson in which the teaching section is led by you, the facilitator, rather than by video. Please spend time going over the material in this lesson during the week before you are scheduled to present this lesson.

+ The illustrations and *Putting It into Practice* segments are available on DVD 3.

+ If you, as the instructor, have any appropriate personal anecdotes that enhance or illustrate the points made in this lesson and honor the Lord, please feel free to add them as you go along.

+ We have provided multiple Bible passages to read and study throughout these facilitator-led sessions. The verses in parentheses are supplemental to the primary verses and may be read as you have time (otherwise, encourage participants to read them during the following week).

+ For the sake of time, you may want to write the passage references given throughout the lesson on individual slips of paper beforehand and pass them out to participants, asking them to read their assigned passage at the appropriate time. Or you may want to have everyone turn to the passage being discussed. The decision is left to you.

Objectives

At the end of this lesson, participants should be able to:

+ Describe the responsibility that children have within the family relationship.

+ Distinguish between a decision that encourages a child-run or a parent-run home.

Getting Started

 Welcome participants to class, open in prayer, make announcements, etc.

In this session we'll be reminding ourselves of the role our children are to fill in our families. It is easy for us to get caught up in raising and providing for our children and to forget that *we* are given the authority over them. For example, have you ever heard parents say (or said yourself) something like, "Well, we'd like to do such-and-such, but our children prefer to do this-and-that?"

Who is really making the decisions for the family in this situation?

Lesson

ILLUSTRATION 5-00

Now that we have taken the time to reflect on our responsibilities as husband and wife, let's look at our responsibilities as parents, and the responsibilities of our children. These principles are fairly cut-and-dry; the challenge is living them out.

A. Children are to obey and honor their parents

ILLUSTRATION 5-01

 Read Exodus 20:12; Proverbs 1:8-9, 3:11-12, 22:6; Ephesians 6:1-3 and Colossians 3:20

What commands are given to children in these verses?

> Answer: Children are specifically called to
>
> · honor their father and mother.
>
> · listen to instruction from their father and mother.
>
> · accept the Lord's discipline and rebuke.
>
> · learn from their parents.
>
> · obey their parents in the Lord.

Notice that the child's training and instruction are to come primarily from his parents. Just as fathers are to be subject to God and mothers are to be subject to their husbands, so children are to be under their parents' authority.

B. Children are sinners

ILLUSTRATION 5-02

Let's review some important truths from last session:

 Read Psalm 51:1-6; Romans 3:9-18 and 1 John 1:8

What do these passages teach about us and our children?

> Answer: Allow participants to discuss that these verses show that we are not born "inherently good," but are all born sinners in rebellion against God. This applies to everyone—young and old, male and female. We are deceiving ourselves if we think that we do not have to contend with a sin nature in ourselves, our spouse or our children. You may want to address the claim that many have, "But they're so cute!"

The reason children disobey is because they are born enslaved to their sinful nature. Foolishness is bound up in their hearts, which is why you as the parent must expect and enforce obedience.

C. Parents are to be the authority in the home

ILLUSTRATION 5-03

The Bible clearly teaches that the home is to be structured so that the parents have authority over the children. Yet in many homes, the child seems to be the center of the household while his parents continually cater to his every need and whim.

Watch *Putting It into Practice—Child-centered homes*.

Let's think for a moment about how we run our households. In what ways might we (perhaps unknowingly) allow our children to have a position of authority?

Answer: Allow participants to discuss this briefly.

ILLUSTRATION 5-04

Although John Charles Ryle wrote this over 100 years ago, his sentiments are still true for today.

> You will see many in this day who allow their children to choose and think for themselves long before they are able, and even make excuses for their disobedience, as if it were a thing not to be blamed. To my eyes, a parent always yielding, and a child always having its own way, are a most painful sight—painful, because I see God's appointed order of things inverted and turned upside down—painful, because I feel sure the consequence to that child's character in the end will be self-will, pride, and self-conceit. You must not wonder that men refuse to obey their Father which is in heaven, if you allow them, when children, to disobey their father who is upon earth.[1]

Let's think for a moment about the choices that we give our children. Is this practice showing them that *we* are in authority over them and teaching them to submit to authority, or is it giving them authority that they shouldn't have?

Answer: Allow participants to discuss this briefly.

D. We are all under authority

ILLUSTRATION 5-05

As a reminder, the concept of submission to authority is found throughout the Bible. The events of Genesis 3 are a clear testimony to what happens when we reject the ultimate authority—God.

We need to be training our children to be under authority so that they will learn to submit to their Creator and to the other authorities that the Lord has given them. Let's briefly look at some of them.

 Read Romans 13:1–7; 1 Corinthians 16:16–18; Ephesians 5:24; Titus 3:1–2; Hebrews 12:9, 13:7; James 4:7; 1 Peter 2:13–18, 5:5–6. As you read, make a list of the authorities that God has ordained over us: government rulers, those who punish

---

[1]   John Charles Ryle, *The Duties of Parents*, 1888

wrongdoers, church leaders, God, Christ, those older than we are, those in positions of authority over us at work.

In a later session, we'll be looking at what God has said we are to do when our children do not fulfill their responsibilities. For now, let's endeavor to keep in mind that God has entrusted our children to us and we are to be ministers of His grace in bringing the good news to our children in both our words and our actions. We can do this by willingly embracing the responsibilities God has given to us and by living out those responsibilities in front of our children and modeling for them the standard which they must live up to. When we each accept the responsibility given to us by the Lord, we are pleasing Him and, by His grace, we will have peace in our homes.

Bringing It Home

1. In previous sessions, Ken mentioned the wisdom of fathers leading their family in scheduled worship times. What practices have you established in order to teach your children about things of the Lord?

 Watch *Putting It into Practice—Family Devotions* for some other ideas about when and how you can implement a family worship time into your lives.

2. As you reflect on the characteristics of godly husbands/fathers and wives/ mothers that we listed during this and the previous session, think about how you are training your children to someday fill these roles. How can you begin *now* to instill the ability to, for example, "manage a home" into your children who will someday (if the Lord wills) be raising children of their own?

3. Along these lines, what are you teaching your children about what the Bible says about marriage, whom they should marry and how they are to find a spouse?

 Watch *Putting It into Practice—Finding a spouse*.

Frequently Asked Question

1. When I fail to obey God, should I reveal my error to my children? Won't this undermine their trust in my authority?

    As important as it is to behave in a manner that glorifies God before our children, we also need to know how to handle those times when we fail to live up to God's standard of holiness (and those times will come—we are all sons and daughters of Adam and Eve!). We need to be willing to repent and seek forgiveness from God and our children.

    Think of a recent time when you sinned against your spouse or children. How did you handle the situation? Could you have handled it in a more Christ-like manner?

Watch *Putting It into Practice—Parental transparency*.

 Close in prayer, and briefly go over the homework assignment with participants.

Homework

This week, evaluate your home life. In what ways have you allowed your children to gain authority over you? What practices do you need to change or modify so that you, as the parents, are the authority, rather than your children?

For More Information

+ *Shepherding a Child's Heart* by Tedd Tripp

  The things your child does and says flow from the heart (Luke 6:45). Written for parents with children of any age, this insightful book provides perpsectives and procedures for shepherding your child's heart into the paths of life.

+ *The Heart of Anger* by Lou Priolo

  Is anger ever a problem in your home? Do your children ever speak to you in angry, disrespectful tones? Do they ever fight between themselves? Have you ever lost your patience and composure when dealing with an infuriating situation in the home? If you honestly answered "yes" to any of these questions, this book is for you. This book deals with anger's root causes, offering corrective advice from a biblical perspective.

Devotional ideas

+ *A Faith to Grow On* by John MacArthur

  This devotional book for children contains important things they should know about God, the Bible, prayer and heaven. Children will receive biblical insights they can actually understand, answers they can count on and the help they want to keep growing closer to God.

+ *Beginnings (Answers in Genesis)*

This curriculum provides answers to foundational questions of the Christian faith: Where did God come from? How did we get the Bible? How old is the earth? Did God create in six actual days? What about the "dating" methods?

+ *The 7 C's of History (Answers in Genesis)*

This curriculum introduces the foundational events of biblical history in seven fun lessons: Creation, Corruption (the Fall of man), Catastrophe (Noah's Flood), Confusion (the Tower of Babel), Christ, Cross and Consummation (the new heavens and new Earth).

+ *Pilgrim's Progress all-in-one curriculum*

This large-format book contains the entire original text of *The Pilgrim's Progress* with John Bunyan's own Scripture annotations, plus a special photo-illustrated section about the man who penned this classic. Within its illustrated pages are "Truths to Ponder" for young children and "Digging Deeper" questions for older students and adults. It also includes activity ideas, character studies and commentary regarding the unique figures that Christian encounters during his journey to the Celestial City.

DISCIPLINE: PRODUCING A HARVEST OF PEACE AND RIGHTEOUSNESS

You will need DVD 3 for this lesson

Overview

As we look to the Scriptures for our parenting guidelines, we find that there are far more verses on discipline than any other subject. This is especially relevant given the negative undertones associated with discipline in our modern society. We should take care to understand how God has told us to correct our children.

In this lesson, we'll discuss why we need to discipline our children and what a Bible-based discipline session may look like. Although the climate of our culture today is such that spanking is generally frowned upon, we'll see that the Bible commands parents to lovingly use "the rod" as a means to train their children to be obedient to the commands of God.

Preparing for the Lesson

This is the third lesson in which the teaching section is led by you, the facilitator, rather than by video. Please spend time going over the material in this lesson during the week before you are scheduled to present this lesson.

+ The illustrations and *Putting It into Practice* segments are available on DVD 3.

+ If you, as the instructor, have any appropriate personal anecdotes that enhance or illustrate the points made in this lesson and honor the Lord, please feel free to add them as you go along.

+ We have provided multiple Bible passages to read and study throughout these facilitator-led sessions. The verses in parentheses are supplemental to the other verses and may be read as you have time (otherwise, encourage participants to read them during the following week).

+ For the sake of time, you may want to write the passage references given throughout the lesson on individual slips of paper beforehand and pass them out to participants, asking them to read their assigned passage at the appropriate time. Or you may want to have everyone turn to the passage being discussed. The decision is left to you.

Objectives

At the end of this lesson, participants will be able to:

+ Explain why discipline is necessary and profitable for our children.

+ Explain when and how to administer discipline.

+ Contrast biblical discipline with abuse.

Getting Started

 Welcome participants to class, open in prayer, make announcements, etc.

Discipline is an area that many parents struggle with, sometimes unknowingly. In this session, we'll be discussing what the Bible has to say about this important topic. Let's begin by considering the following question.

1. What comes to mind when you think of "discipline"?

2. How many times in the past week have you said to your children something like, "I've had it up to here with your behavior!" or "Don't make me tell you one more time to pick up your toys!"

Lesson

ILLUSTRATION 6-00

We'll begin this session by looking at the need for discipline.

 Read Ephesians 6:1 (Colossians 3:20)

We saw in the lesson on the responsibilities of children that they are to obey their parents in the Lord. As we all know, the reason children are commanded to obey is because they are, by nature, disobedient.

A. The problem

1. Our children are sinners

ILLUSTRATION 6-01

 Read Psalm 51:5 (Romans 3:10–18; 5:12)

We inherited a sinful nature from our father, Adam. In turn, our children inherited it from us. The reason we're having this discussion on how to raise godly children is because our first parents did *not* obey the directive of the Creator in the beginning. Since that time, humanity has been in continual rebellion against the Lord and His word. Our children, cute as they may be, are born in slavery to their sinful flesh.

Suppose someone comments to you that children are born "blank slates," that is, with no predisposition to good or evil. How would you respond?

> Answer: Children are born enslaved to their sinful nature. This means that they are naturally self-centered, disobedient and foolish. Therefore, training is necessary to correct this natural direction.

2. Foolishness is bound up in the hearts of our children

 Read Proverbs 22:15

ILLUSTRATION 6-02

Foolishness is "bound up" in the hearts of our children. This does not mean they are stupid—quite the opposite, as any parent of young children quickly discovers. Their little minds are capable of astonishingly creative thinking and accurate information recall. To what, then, does this "foolishness" refer?

According to the Baker's *Evangelical Dictionary of Biblical Theology,*

> The heaviest concentration of the Hebrew words referring to foolishness is in the Wisdom literature, where the fool is constantly contrasted with the wise. The fool is not so much stupid (except when the context demands such a meaning) as immoral and pernicious.

The fool's problem is not so much intellectual as practical and spiritual. In fact, the terms "wise" and "fool" are used by the sages to designate respectively the faithful and the sinners. … A further insight into the nature of the fool is provided by the Hebrew word *nabal*. This is the word used in Psalm 14:1, where the fool declares, "There is no God."[1]

Foolishness, then, manifests itself in our children in their disobedience and disrespect for authority. What are some specific ways children manifest this foolishness?

> Answer: Discuss some examples of deliberate disobedience in both action and attitudes. For example,
>
> · When called to "come," the child turns and walks or crawls the other way.
> · When told "no," the child begins to whine, complain, talk-back or argue.
> · When told "no," the child continues to reach his hand toward the forbidden, but desired, object.
> · When a baby struggles against having his diaper changed.

According the Bible, when our children manifest such foolish behavior, it becomes necessary for us to discipline them. Although this may have negative connotations to some people, we need to be willing to submit ourselves to what the Creator has told us to do. So let's look at what the Bible says about discipline.

B. Disciplining your children

1. We need to have the proper motivation

ILLUSTRATION 6-03

 Read Proverbs 3:11–12 and Hebrews 12:5–11 (Revelation 3:19)

Our Creator disciplines His children when they disobey His commands. Notice that the motivation for God's discipline is His love for them—His desire to do what is best for them. And for those who are trained by it, discipline yields the peaceful fruit of righteousness. It causes them to become more like Christ—holy and completely obedient to the will of the Father.

Likewise, the motivation behind the discipline of our children must be love. We should mourn over the foolishness bound up in their hearts and desire to instill in them a reverence for God's holiness to the end that they might come to a deep repentance over their sin, seeking forgiveness in Christ and working out their salvation with fear and trembling (Philippians 2:12). The prayer is that by learning to be obedient to their parents, children will learn to be obedient to God and the authorities He has established over them.

---

[1]   Edited by Walter A. Elwell, published by Baker Books, Grand Rapids, Michigan

2. **We need to expect biblical obedience**

    ILLUSTRATION 6-04

     Read Romans 1:28-31 (2 Timothy 3:1-5; Titus 1:6)

    God puts a high priority on children obeying their parents; note how "disobedient to their parents" is listed among other grievous sins against God such as greed, strife and murder. And having disobedient children is sufficient to disqualify a man from being an elder in the church.

    ILLUSTRATION 6-05

    John Charles Ryle wrote in 1888:

    > Parents, determine to make your children obey you—though it may cost you much trouble—and cost them many tears! Let there be no questioning, and reasoning, and disputing, and delaying, and answering back. When you give them a command, let them see plainly that you will have it done. … Where, in deed, is the honour which the fifth commandment enjoins, if fathers and mothers are not obeyed cheerfully, willingly, and at once?[2]

    We need to avoid delay tactics when a child disobeys, such as counting to ten, saying "if you do that again…" or raising our voice to show that we *really* mean it this time. When we do these things, we are training them that obedience is only necessary under certain circumstances (only when you reach nine-and-a-half, only the third time or only when that vein starts bulging on the side on your neck). We are, in effect, training our children to believe that the words of an authority don't matter.

    Expecting obedience with a biblical attitude will provide ample opportunities for correction and instruction. Think about how you are training your children—do you require them to obey you immediately and cheerfully, or are you allowing them to continue in sins (such as selfishness, pride, laziness or complaining) that displease the Lord?

3. **We need to use the rod**

    ILLUSTRATION 6-06

     Read Proverbs 13:24 and 23:13-14 (Proverbs 10:13, 22:15, 29:15)

    When your children disobey God's commands, you (as the parent) are instructed to discipline them. One of the primary tools that the Creator has commanded us to use for disciplining our children is the rod. The Hebrew word for "rod" describes

---

[2] John Charles Ryle, *The Duties of Parents*, 1888

what we might call a cane, stick, switch or paddle.[3] Let's look in more detail at what a discipline session using the rod might look like.

C. Suggested elements for a fruit-producing discipline session

We need to keep in mind that discipline aims to produce the "peaceful fruit of righteousness" in the one being disciplined. This often means that a discipline session will take time. A typical discipline session might consist of the following elements:

ILLUSTRATION 6-07

1. Have a proper attitude

Remember, discipline is an act of love (Proverbs 13:24) as we rescue our children from the destructive path of disobedience to the commands of God (Proverbs 23:13–14). If you are angry, frustrated or vengeful in any way, *stop*. Wait until you calm down. Enlist the help of your spouse if possible and appropriate.

ILLUSTRATION 6-08

2. Seek privacy

It is recommended that parents take care to administer discipline in a private area where they can be alone with their child.

ILLUSTRATION 6-09

3. Generate an understanding of the specific offense in the child and explain that he has offended his Creator God

Communicate to your child the specific reason for the spanking. Was it disobedience, selfishness, complaining, etc.? Discuss with your child why what he did was wrong, what the correct behavior looks like and what God expects from us (as revealed in His Word). Engage him in a conversation about his disobedience and why he is being corrected as you lead him toward repentance.

Many times we, as parents, can feel wronged or injured by our child's foolish behavior. However, we need to keep in mind that the greater offense is against the Creator who has set forth the commands that have been violated. Disobedience is wrong, not because it interferes with our plans, but because God has commanded children to obey their parents (Ephesians 6:1–3). Complaining is wrong, not because it an-

---

[3] It has become fashionable in some Christian circles to evade the Bible's clear teaching of physical punishment by claiming that the rod merely refers to a staff used by shepherds to lead their sheep in the right direction. Thus, we are to "guide" our child to righteousness through the use of a metaphorical "rod." But clearly (Proverbs 23:13–14) the rod is intended as an instrument to inflict discomfort for the sake of rescuing our child's soul. We must not alter our hermeneutics based on the social acceptability of the Scripture's commands.

noys us, but because God has commanded us to do everything without complaining (Philippians 2:14).

ILLUSTRATION 6-10

Tedd Tripp, author of *Shepherding a Child's Heart,* emphasizes this point:

> The rod underscores the importance of obeying God. Remember the issue is never, "You have failed to obey ME." The only reason for a child to obey Mom and Dad is that God commands it. Failure to obey Mom or Dad is, therefore, failure to obey God. This is the issue. The child has failed to obey God. The child has failed to do what God has mandated. To persist places the child at great risk. It is not a kindness for the parent to ignore the rebellion against God's authority that will ultimately bring God's even greater chastisement.[4]

Lovingly share with him that you must correct his disobedience because to do otherwise would mean you were being disobedient to God.

ILLUSTRATION 6-11

4. **Lovingly administer the correction**

ILLUSTRATION 6-12

Regarding the actual spanking, Tedd Tripp states:

> The rod is the careful, timely, measured and controlled use of physical punishment. The rod is never a venting of parental anger. It is not what the parent does when he is frustrated. It is not a response to feeling that his child has made things hard for him. It is always measured and controlled. The parent knows the proper measure of severity for this particular child at this particular time. The child knows how many swats are to come.[4]

ILLUSTRATION 6-13

5. **Seek reconciliation and restoration**

As you bring the discipline session to a close, make sure that you don't leave while the child is still crying. Take great care to hold and hug him and teach him that while his disobedience broke the fellowship you have with each other, the discipline and repentance enables you to be reconciled and peace to be restored. Express your love for your child and be careful to tell him that you want only the best for him. Pray with him and as the Lord leads, use this opportunity to talk with your child about

---

[4]   Tedd Tripp, *Shepherding a Child's Heart,* Shepherd Press, 2005, p. 106.

how we can be restored to fellowship with our Creator through the death and resurrection of Christ Jesus.

 Read 2 Corinthians 5:18–21

This is an aspect that many non-biblical disciplinary methods miss. When we put our children in "time-out" or ground them for a week, the punishment continues for however long without bringing the child back into fellowship with their God and their parents. We need to carefully evaluate what we are trying to accomplish when we discipline our children.

ILLUSTRATION 6-14

Let's look at this quote that discusses how to wrap up a discipline session:

> The time a parent spends with his or her children after a spanking will also help confirm to the parent that the child's heart has truly been brought to repentance. If steps of restitution are necessary, the child can be instructed in this at this time. If they have shown a wrong attitude toward someone, they should go to that person and say, "I'm sorry. Will you forgive me?" If they disobeyed in some way, they will need to go back and do what they were asked to do. This will bring children back into a positive direction of obedience and proper attitude.[5]

As we've seen in this session, one important aspect of training children to be godly is instilling in them a spirit of cheerful obedience and disciplining them lovingly and appropriately when they are not obedient. Next week, we'll look at another important aspect of training and discipline—communication.

---

[5]   Roy Lessin, *Spanking—A Loving Discipline*, Bethany House Publishers, 2002, p. 75.

Bringing It Home

1. One common objection to the biblically-mandated use of the rod when disciplining children is "But I love my child too much to spank him." What does the Bible say about the relationship between loving our children and disciplining them?

2. Many people object to using "the rod" to discipline their children because they believe it is child abuse. What does biblical discipline look like? And how does it differ from abuse?

 Watch *Putting It into Practice—Biblical discipline vs. abuse*.

3. One aspect of the discipline process that can tend to exasperate children is a lack of consistency on the parents' part. Why do you think this may be true?

    A lack of consistency can also lead to ineffective discipline. Explain why you think this may be true.

    What are some steps that you can take to become more consistent in disciplining your children?

4. An important part of the discipline process is that it be done in a controlled manner, and not out of anger or a sense of vengeance. Inevitably, however, because we all still struggle with the "old man," we will get angry. What are some steps we can take to ensure that we don't discipline while we're angry?

5. Some parents claim, "I've tried spanking, and my child just doesn't seem to respond. Should I try something else?" What does the Bible teach us about this?

 Watch *Putting It into Practice—Why won't my children listen?*

 Close in prayer, and briefly go over the homework assignment with participants.

Frequently Asked Questions

For more detailed answers to questions such as the following, we refer you to Tedd Tripp's book *Shepherding a Child's Heart.*

1. Is there a difference between foolishness and acts of childishness?

    Certainly. Children are prone to accidents and lack the ability to accomplish some tasks. For example, it would be unreasonable to discipline your child for accidentally knocking over a glass of juice or failing to obey your command to recite the first 100 prime numbers. A wise parent will learn to discern between deliberate disobedience and childish behavior.

2. Where and how hard should I spank my child?

    John MacArthur in *Successful Christian Parenting* says that pain inflicted during a spanking is "designed not to injure the child, but to make the consequences of disobedience unforgettable. If your spanking leaves bruises or welts that are still visible the following day, you are striking the child too hard. Short, stinging strokes to the backside (where the natural padding is most plentiful), will not injure the child, but should be painful enough to make the consequences of disobedience sufficiently distasteful and unforgettable."[6]

3. Should my children be allowed to appeal if they disagree with a command?

---

[6]   John MacArthur, *Successful Christian Parenting,* p. 85.

You may want to teach your children how to respectfully disagree with something you have asked of them, as long as they are willing to accept your biblically-based answer as the final authority once their appeal has been heard.

4. Inevitably, children will misbehave while you are in public, for example, while grocery shopping or at the library. Because of society's views on biblical discipline, it is probably not the wisest course to administer a discipline session at the time of the misbehavior, and yet it must be corrected. What are some ways you can handle disobedience that occurs while you're out and about?

Answer: It may be best to leave the store and head home immediately in order to address the child's offense, rather than trying to administer discipline in the store or in the car. Parents need to keep in mind that their primary task is training their children, not getting the grocery shopping finished or checking out the library books. We need to be willing to put aside what we want to do in order to make sure our children understand what the Lord desires of them.

Homework

1. Ever since the first act of disobedience by Adam and Eve, the Lord has been correcting wayward sinners. This week, read the book of Jonah, which describes how the Lord dealt with one man's disobedience.

2. One of the chief causes of ineffective discipline is a lack of harmony between parents concerning the discipline of their children. This week, sit down with your spouse and prayerfully discuss ways that you can show a "united front" in this crucial area. Are you in agreement on what behaviors or attitudes you will discipline for? How can you help each other become more accountable and consistent in lovingly rescuing your children from the path of destruction?

3. Continue working on drafting a family mission statement that will help you and your spouse to parent your children. What does the Creator want for your children? What verses can you use to guide you?

For More Information

* *Shepherding a Child's Heart* by Tedd Tripp

   The things your child does and says flow from the heart (Luke 6:45). Written for parents with children of any age, this insightful book provides perpsectives and procedures for shepherding your child's heart into the paths of life.

* *Spanking—A Loving Discipline* by Roy Lessin

   For all Christian parents who wonder how to discipline their young children, Roy Lessin clearly explains the biblical mandate to "train children in the way they should go" and how spanking is one part of that mandate. Lessin teaches parents when and how to spank in a way that helps children learn to obey. Just as important, he teaches when not to spank, including a straightforward, helpful distinction between loving discipline and child abuse.

+ *"Don't Make Me Count to Three!"* by Ginger Plowman

Do you find yourself threatening, repeating your instructions or raising your voice in an attempt to get your children to obey? Are you discouraged because it seems you just can't reach the heart of your child? Through personal experience and practical application of Scripture, Ginger Plowman encourages and equips moms to reach past the outward behavior of their children and dive deeply into the issues of the heart. Ginger's candid approach will help moms move beyond the frustrations of not knowing how to handle issues of disobedience and into a confident, well-balanced approach to raising their children.

+ *Age of Opportunity: A Biblical Guide to Parenting Teens* by Paul Tripp

From the argument over the last donut, to the cry of "nothing to wear" a half-hour before school, Paul Tripp uncovers the heart issues affecting parents and their teenagers during the often chaotic adolescent years. He shows parents how to seize the countless opportunities to deepen communication, learn and grow with their teenagers.

COMMUNICATING BIBLICALLY WITH YOUR CHILDREN

You will need DVD 3 for this lesson

Overview

In the previous lesson, we discussed the importance of lovingly disciplining our children as we bring them up in the nurture and admonition of the Lord. An important aspect of loving discipline is communicating to our children what they have done wrong and how they can correct it. However, communicating the truths of Scripture with our children should not be limited to the discipline process, but should pervade every area of our lives as we seek to develop in them a love for God and His Word.

During this session, we will be discussing various aspects of how the Creator wants us to share His truth with our children (and others!). We will look at some of the defining characteristics of communication that honor the Lord and discuss the importance of using biblical terminology to define and correct sinful patterns of behavior. We will be challenging the participants to evaluate their current communication practices and encouraging them to conform to what the Lord desires of us.

Preparing for the Lesson

This is the fourth lesson in which the teaching section is led by you, the facilitator, rather than by video. Please spend time going over the material in this lesson during the week before you are scheduled to present this lesson.

+ The illustrations and *Putting It into Practice* segments are available on DVD 3.

- If you, as the instructor, have any appropriate personal anecdotes that enhance or illustrate the points made in this lesson and honor the Lord, please feel free to add them as you go along.

- We have provided multiple Bible passages to read and study throughout these facilitator-led sessions. The verses in parentheses are supplemental to the other verses and may be read as you have time (otherwise, encourage participants to read them during the following week).

- For the sake of time, you may want to write the passage references given throughout the lesson on individual slips of paper beforehand and pass them out to participants, asking them to read their assigned passage at the appropriate time. Or you may want to have everyone turn to the passage being discussed. The decision is left to you.

Objectives

At the end of this lesson, participants should be able to:

- Explain why it is important to communicate biblically.

- Define sins and virtues using biblical terminology.

- Identify teaching moments in everyday life using the "Deuteronomy 6" principle.

- Initiate a plan to evaluate the unique struggles of each of your children.

- Identify biblical (and unbiblical) attitudes in our speech patterns.

Getting Started

 Welcome participants to class, open in prayer, make announcements, etc.

In this session, we'll be looking at what the Bible says about communicating in a way that honors the Lord and applying this to how we train our children. First, however, let's consider a few examples of how people can communicate.

1. Have you ever experienced a parent belittling or screaming at their child in public, such as in the grocery store? What went through your mind at the time? How did it make you feel to watch the situation?

2. Suppose your six-year-old son is constantly pushing his younger sister. What is the difference between saying "Well, boys will be boys" and saying he has a problem with a "violent spirit"?

Lesson

ILLUSTRATION 7-00

In many ways, all Christians are in the business of communication. After all, it is through the "foolishness of the message preached" that God saves those who believe (1 Corinthians 1:21, NASB). And we know that all of Scripture is "profitable for teaching, for reproof, for correction, for training in righteousness; so that the man of God may be adequate, equipped for every good work" (2 Timothy 3:16–17, NASB).

Our words can also destroy ourselves and others—"the tongue is set among our members as that which defiles the entire body" (James 3:6, NASB). The same member of our bodies capable of sharing the saving grace of Christ can be just as effective in propagating false doctrine and slander.

We need to remember that the way we communicate with our children will profoundly impact their worldview. Let's begin this session by looking at what the Bible teaches us about *how* we are to communicate.

A. How to communicate

ILLUSTRATION 7-01

1. **Use gentleness, sweetness of speech**

 Read Galatians 5:25–6:4 and Proverbs 16:21 (Ephesians 4:29; Colossians 4:6; 1 Corinthians 13:4–7)

A believer's speech should be characterized by "gentleness" (Galatians 6:1, NASB), "sweetness of speech" (Proverbs 16:21, NASB) and "with grace, as though seasoned with salt" (Colossians 4:6, NASB). This is especially important to remember as we converse with our children, since their communication patterns will be profoundly influenced by how we communicate with them. It is easy, especially when they are disobeying us for the tenth time in an hour, to slip into fleshly patterns of speech. (But then, you weren't keeping a record of wrongs, were you?) What are some such sinful patterns that we can exhibit?

Answer: Allow participants to respond. Galatians mentions being boastful, challenging (in the sense of prideful) and envious. We might also respond in anger, yell, use sarcasm (i.e., have a "holier-than-thou" attitude), be vindictive, etc.

Read James 1:20

James specifically notes that "the anger of man does not achieve the righteousness of God" (NASB). Fruit-bearing children are not grown from the fertilizer of fearing angry, vindictive parents.

ILLUSTRATION 7-02

2. **Use both reproof and encouragement**

 Read 1 Thessalonians 2:11–12 and 1 Thessalonians 5:11 (Romans 1:8; Philippians 1:3–5)

We need to take care that we are not only reproving and rebuking our children, but that we are also encouraging and praising what is good. When your children exhibit obedience to God's commands, be quick to point it out to them, especially if it is something with which they have been struggling. If your normally selfish three-year-old suddenly one morning asks your six-year-old if he would like the larger bowl of cereal, celebrate that he is considering others more important than himself!

ILLUSTRATION 7-03

3. **Listen and observe**

 Read James 1:19–20 (Proverbs 10:19, 18:13)

We need to remember that communicating with our children (or with anyone, for that matter) involves speaking as well as listening. It's easy to slip into a pattern of talking *at* our children, rather than talking *with* them. Without listening and observation, we may not be aware of the sinful behaviors that are unique to each child. As we make a conscious effort to do this, eventually it will become a habit for us, and enable us to evaluate and respond to our children in a more effective way.

ILLUSTRATION 7-04

B. **Where and when to communicate: The Deuteronomy 6 principle**

 Read Deuteronomy 6:4–9

Communicating biblically with our children should not be confined to formal family devotional times and discipline sessions. We are encouraged to speak of the things of the Lord throughout the day and wherever we might find ourselves. Oftentimes it is those Spirit-led informal teaching sessions, during the otherwise routine events of life, that sink deepest into the heart.

To see an expert in this principle, we have only to carefully study the books of Matthew, Mark, Luke and John. Our Messiah constantly drew analogies and used His physical surroundings, historical events, circumstances, comments from the crowd, etc.

Watch *Putting It into Practice—the Deuteronomy 6 principle*.

Let's discuss some practical ways that we can keep the commands of Christ as part of our discussion throughout the day.

> Answer: Allow participants to respond. At its simplest, objects can remind us of biblical lessons (for example, a rainbow for Noah's flood; a supermarket for Jesus feeding the crowds). Others may be more abstract; there is really no end to the possibilities.

ILLUSTRATION 7-05

C. What to communicate: Using biblical vocabulary

 Read 2 Timothy 3:16 (Psalm 19:7–11)

As we think about striving to communicate biblical principles with our children, we may think the Bible has little to say about certain situations. This may be because we fail to define the problem in biblical terms. For example, you will look in vain for the verse on "not eating broccoli." In such situations, try to define the problem biblically:

+ Is the exhibited behavior symptomatic of a particular sin?

+ Is there a biblical synonym that I can look up in a concordance?

When we define our broccoli problem biblically (perhaps "selfish," "ungrateful," "finding fault" or simply "disobedient"), we can look those words up in a concordance and apply biblical wisdom. We can also show these verses to our children so that they understand that it is *God's* commands they are disobeying.

The same principle applies to praising our children. If we define their positive characteristics in biblical terms, we can show them through the Scripture how they are obeying God.

Training our minds (and our children's minds) to think in biblical terms also protects us from being deceived by euphemisms[1] that distort biblical truth. For example, pride (Proverbs 11:2) is called "self-esteem;" Someone is "blunt; forthright; tell-it-like-it-is" instead of guilty of "harsh words" (Proverbs 15:1).

 Read Ephesians 4:22–25 (Colossians 3:8–12)

The Bible speaks of the Christian walk in terms of "putting off" the old nature and "putting on" the new nature. We can apply this same principle in training our children. Instead of continually saying "don't do that," we can explain the sinful behavior or at-

---

1   "Euphemism" is the substitution of a milder term to replace one that might be considered offensive. At times, this can help us be gentle in our speech. However, more often than not they are used to mislead ("used cars" are "pre-owned cars"; abortion advocates are "pro-choice.")

titude that they need to "put off," why it displeases the Lord, and then teach them the alternative behavior that they need to "put on." Ephesians 4:25 provides one example: we are to lay aside falsehood ("put off") and instead speak truth ("put on").

You will have a chance to practice these concepts in the "Bringing It Home" section.

D. Why we need to use biblical vocabulary

ILLUSTRATION 7-06

 Read John 17:17 and 2 Timothy 3:15-17 (Hebrews 4:12; 1 Peter 1:23)

Regeneration and sanctification are the work of the Holy Spirit in the lives of our children, and so we need to be continually pleading with Him to save and sanctify our children (John 3:6–7; 2 Thessalonians 2:13). However, one of the primary means that He uses to effect change in our lives and in the lives of our children is through the Word of God. Thus, we must take care that both the content (what we are saying) and the attitude (how we are saying it) of our speech be grounded in Scripture. Our goal should be that this rich indwelling of the Word of Christ (Colossians 3:16) will equip our children to think and communicate biblically as they mature and eventually go out on their own.

 Read Galatians 5:13–18 and 1 John 5:2-4 (Joshua 22:4-6; Psalm 119:167; John 14:15; Colossians 3:15-17)

We do not want to raise children capable of obeying only man-made systems of rules and regulations, or children who obey to gain the approval of others. The effective Christian life is characterized by obedience to Christ's commands motivated by a love for God, directed by communion with the indwelling Holy Spirit. This type of obedience comes from a thorough understanding of the Scripture.

ILLUSTRATION 7-07

The late Dr. Henry Morris remarked,

> The godly man does not arrive at spiritual maturity instantaneously.
> It is a lifelong process, but **every stage of that growth must come from the Word.**[2] (emphasis added)

In this session, we can only hope to scratch the tip of the surface of this subject; we would encourage you to study and meditate on this more on your own time.

---

2   Dr. Henry Morris, *Treasures in the Psalms*, Master Books, 2000, p. 118.

Bringing It Home

1. Let's apply what we've been learning above to a hypothetical situation where your child is whining. Think of a situation which might incite whining.

   What is the biblical terminology for the child's behavior?

   What are some relevant verses?

   How would you communicate to your child what he has done wrong?

2. Your child does not obey your command to clean his room. Name a biblical way and an unbiblical way you might respond.

3. Around the dinner table with your family, you are discussing a decision at work that you disagree with. Name a biblical way and an unbiblical way you might converse.

4. Choose a few of the following experiences that might be common to your everyday life and brainstorm ways to apply the "Deuteronomy 6" principle.

   + Gardening
   + Passing by a homeless shelter
   + When something breaks
   + Mowing the grass
   + Grocery shopping
   + Overhearing a harsh conversation

5. The chart at the end of this session contains a number of specific manifestations of problems you may have with your children. Try to define them biblically, name the "put on" alternative and list some relevant Scripture references. You can do some during this session, and complete the chart (and add more) for homework.

 Close in prayer, and briefly go over the homework assignment with participants.

Homework

1. Review the verses included in the lesson that you did not have time to read during class. Write down the principles in each one and indicate how you might apply them in your parenting.

2. For each of your children, list three qualities for which you can praise them. Define the qualities biblically, make note of the Bible references that highlight these qualities, and describe specifically how your child is being obedient to the Creator's commands. Make plans to communicate this praise to them. Pray with your children, asking the Lord to continue developing these characteristics in their lives. Every few months, review this list and revise as needed.

3. For each of your children, list three qualities with which they are struggling. Define the qualities biblically, make note of the Bible references that highlight these qualities, and describe specifically how your child is being disobedient to God's commands. Plan to share this with them the next time they exhibit this behavior during your discipline session. Pray with your children, asking the Lord to help them to change in these areas. Every few months, review this list and revise as needed.

4. Continue working on drafting a family mission statement that will help you and your spouse to parent your children. What does the Creator want for your children? What verses can you use to guide you?

For More Information

+ *Shepherding a Child's Heart* by Tedd Tripp

   The things your child does and says flow from the heart (Luke 6:45). Written for parents with children of any age, this insightful book provides perpsectives and procedures for shepherding your child's heart into the paths of life.

+ *"Don't Make Me Count to Three!"* by Ginger Plowman

   Do you find yourself threatening, repeating your instructions or raising your voice in an attempt to get your children to obey? Are you discouraged because it seems you just can't reach the heart of your child? Through personal experience and practical application of Scripture, Ginger Plowman helps moms move beyond the frustrations of not knowing how to handle issues of disobedience and into a confident, well-balanced approach to raising their children.

+ *Age of Opportunity: A Biblical Guide to Parenting Teens* by Paul Tripp

From the argument over the last donut, to the cry of "nothing to wear" a half-hour before school, Paul Tripp uncovers the heart issues affecting parents and their teenagers during the often chaotic adolescent years. He shows parents how to seize the countless opportunities to deepen communication, learn and grow with their teenagers.

+ *Teach Them Diligently: How to Use the Scriptures in Child Training* by Lou Priolo

With all of your training, do you really know how to use the Bible for doctrine, reproof, correction and instruction in righteousness with your children? If you don't, this little book will augment and strengthen your parenting skills as you learn how to use the Scriptures more thoroughly and effectively in your child training.

+ *Everyday Talk—Talking Freely and Naturally about God with Your Children* by John A. Younts

This book offers practical, creative ways to carry out the Deuteronomy 6 principle. Learn how to use ordinary conversations to show your kids the goodness and wisdom of God.

+ *Wisdom for Today's Issues: A Topical Arrangement of the Proverbs* by Stephen Voorwinde

Finding all that the Proverbs say on any given topic can be difficult. Yet nothing is more relevant to the issues of our day, and nothing is more needed in an aimless society, than the divinely inspired Proverbs. This handbook is designed to make the Proverbs more accessible to readers today. Every verse in Proverbs is catagorized and printed in full for quick reference.

+ *The Young Peacemaker* by Corlette Sande

This curriculum (which features a leader's guide and student activity books) teaches students to respond to conflict God's way.

Behavior	Biblical characteristic to "put off"	Biblical characteristic to "put on"	Relevant verses
Fights with a sibling over a toy	Selfishness	Counting others more important than self	Philippians 2:3–4; Proverbs 11:24–25; Romans 12:20–21; James 3:13–18 and 1 Peter 4:9–11
Refuses to take a bath	Stubborn; insubordinate	Respectful; obedient; submissive	
Room is constantly messy	Laziness, sluggardness, slothfulness		
Cries when you turn out the lights			
Consistently fails to say "thank you"			
Makes fun of a sibling when that sibling fails			
Does not ever want to stop playing video games			
Consistently provokes a sibling			
Constantly requests something new to do			

Growing a Godly Heritage

You will need DVD 4 for this lesson

Overview

As we've learned in previous sessions, parents (and especially fathers) bear an incredible responsibility in raising and training their children in the nurture and admonition of the Lord. In this lesson, Steve Ham (Ken's youngest brother) outlines four main areas for parents to keep in mind as they raise their children. These are principles that he gleaned from watching how his father handled the Word of Truth. The first is that the Bible is sufficient—God has provided us with everything we need pertaining to life and godliness through the knowledge of His Son (2 Peter 1:3). The second is that the Bible must be our final authority in all areas it touches on. The third is that the Bible provides a comprehensive and accurate view of the world. The fourth is that the Bible must be read exegetically (using the grammatical-historical approach), rather than eisegetically.

Steve ends with the challenging question, "How would *your* children describe your theological system?"

Objectives

At the end of this lesson, participants will be able to:

+   Describe the doctrine of the sufficiency of Scripture.

+   Distinguish between eisegesis and exegesis.

+   Articulate a Bible-based view on teaching children about Santa Claus and the Easter bunny.

Getting Started

 Welcome participants to class, open in prayer, make announcements, etc.

In this session, we'll be hearing from Steve Ham, Ken's youngest brother, about how their father approached the Word of God. Steve describes for us four aspects of Mervyn Ham's theological system.

If asked, how would your children describe your approach to the Word of God?

Growing a Godly Heritage video outline

 Play *Growing a Godly Heritage* DVD.

Steve's family history

Mervyn Ham's theological system

The Bible is sufficient

> Christian Psychology as the term is used today is an oxymoron. The word psychology no longer speaks of studying the soul; instead it describes a diverse menagerie of therapies and theories that are fundamentally humanistic. The presuppositions and most of the doctrine of psychology cannot be successfully integrated with Christian truth. Moreover, the infusion of psychology into the teaching of the church has blurred the line between behavior modification and sanctification. If one is a truly Christian psychologist, he must be doing soul work in the realm of the deep things of the word and spirit—not fooling around in the shallows of behavior modification. (John MacArthur, *Our Sufficiency in Christ*)

Behavior modification vs. sanctification

Romans 12:2

> Do not conform any longer to the pattern of this world, but be transformed by the renewing of your mind. Then you will be able to test and approve what God's will is—his good, pleasing and perfect will. (NIV)

2 Timothy 3:15–17

> ... and how from infancy you have known the holy Scriptures, which are able to make you wise for salvation through faith in Christ Jesus.

All Scripture is God-breathed and is useful for teaching, rebuking, correcting and training in righteousness, so that the man of God may be thoroughly equipped for every good work. (NIV)

The Bible is the final authority on all matters it touches on

1 Timothy 1:3–7

As I urged you when I went into Macedonia, stay there in Ephesus so that you may command certain men not to teach false doctrines any longer nor to devote themselves to myths and endless genealogies. These promote controversies rather than God's work—which is by faith. The goal of this command is love, which comes from a pure heart and a good conscience and a sincere faith. Some have wandered away from these and turned to meaningless talk. They want to be teachers of the law, but they do not know what they are talking about or what they so confidently affirm. (NIV)

God's Word is reliable and credible

Noah's Ark and fairy tales

2 Timothy 2:15

Do your best to present yourself to God as one approved, a workman who does not need to be ashamed and who correctly handles the word of truth. (NIV)

The Bible provides a comprehensive worldview

The Bible must be understood exegetically

Exegesis

Eisegesis

How do your children describe *your* theological system?

Bringing It Home

 Use this time to discuss the following questions with participants. Many of the illustrations used in the video are available on the DVD for you to refer to as necessary.

1. Choose 10 of the following passages to read. Write beside the reference what that passage teaches about the sufficiency of Christ and His Word.

   Deuteronomy 6:4–6

   Deuteronomy 17:18–20

   Job 23:12

Psalm 12:6

Psalm 19:7–11

Jeremiah 15:16

Micah 2:7

Matthew 4:1–11

Mark 12:24

Luke 11:28

Luke 16:19–31

John 17:17

Acts 20:32

1 Corinthians 2:6–16

2 Corinthians 3:5

2 Corinthians 9:8–10

Colossians 2:3–10

Colossians 3:16

1 Thessalonians 2:11–13

2 Timothy 3:15–17

1 Peter 2:2–3

2 Peter 1:1–9

1 John 2:20–27

Revelation 22:18–19

2. Although God uses godly men and women to exhort us concerning things of the Lord, we must never allow any counsel to stand in the place of God's Word in our lives. Read Acts 17:10–12. How did the Bereans handle Paul's teachings?

Think about the advice and counsel that you have received about raising children (and about life in general). Has any of it turned you away from the Word of God and toward the counsel of men? Or has it encouraged you to search the Scriptures more diligently? In what ways? How can you follow the example set by the Berean Christians in the future?

3. Exegesis is defined (by the Random House *Webster's Unabridged Dictionary*) as "critical explanation or interpretation of a text or portion of a text, esp. of the Bible." Eisegesis is defined (by the Random House *Webster's Unabridged Dictionary*) as "an interpretation, esp. of Scripture, that expresses the interpreter's own ideas, bias, or the like, rather than the meaning of the text." Explain in your own words the difference between exegesis and eisegesis.

    Think about the way you usually read and understand Scripture. Are you reading it exegetically or eisegetically?

    Give an example of an eisegetic interpretation of Scripture.

    How can you respond to such eisegetical interpretations?

4. Steve discussed the need to separate Jesus from Santa Claus, the Easter bunny and Winnie the Pooh. Why is this important? How have you taught your children about these figures?

 Watch *Putting It into Practice—Santa Claus and our children* for varying perspectives on this topic.

    In what ways are you making the Bible real to your children, rather than just another book of stories? For example, how have you taught your children about the account of Noah and the Ark, the Tower of Babel, Abraham, the Israelites and Jonah? Have you taught them as real historical people and events, or merely as nice "stories"?

5. Consider Paul's exhortation to Timothy in 1 Timothy 1:3–6. Where have you seen false doctrine interfere with love, conscience and faith?

 Close in prayer, and briefly go over the homework assignment with participants.

Homework

1. During this week, read Proverbs 16–20 with your spouse (we suggest reading one chapter per day). In a journal, write down the insights that both of you glean from these chapters. Additionally, consider the following questions:

   + What do the Proverbs teach about discipline?

   + What does Solomon teach about the nature of children?

   + How does Solomon communicate with his children?

   + Solomon frequently compares the behavior of the wise to the behavior of the foolish. What are the characteristics of the wise? What behaviors characterize the life of the foolish? Make a list of the characteristics of each as you go through this book. Is your life more characteristic of the wise or of the foolish? Because we can do nothing apart from the Lord, ask Him to show you areas in which you need to put off foolish behavior and put on the behavior of the wise. As you pray, ask Him to help you train your children to be wise. Most importantly, pray with an attitude of belief (read James 1:5–6).

2. Finish completing "Bringing It Home" question 1.

3. Read Psalm 119:89–176. What does the psalmist say regarding the sufficiency and authority of Scripture?

4. Some people claim that the Bible's authority should be limited to the faith and moral arena and should not be considered an authority on science or history. How would you respond to such claims? Visit www.AnswersInGenesis.org/go/science for some ideas.

For More Information

+ *How to Read the Bible for All Its Worth* by Gordon D. Fee and Douglas Stuart

  The primary task of Bible study is to determine what the Scriptures meant at the time they were written and how that meaning applies to us today. This vital guide focuses on the historical contexts of the Bible and explains differences between the Old Testament narratives, the Epistles, Gospels, Parables, Psalms and more. It's a practical approach to Bible study.

+ *Exegetical Fallacies* by D.A. Carson

  Assuming that the reader possesses a working knowledge of Greek, this book identifies the common grammatical, lexical, cultural, theological and historical mistakes that Bible exegetes can make.

+ www.AnswersInGenesis.org/go/science

SESSION 9

THE FAMILY FORTRESS

You will need DVD 4 for this lesson

Overview

Certainly we all desire to provide for our children a home that is a "fortress" against the attacks of evil. But in order to do so, we must recognize *who* actually does the building, lest we assume a responsibility that is not our own, or feel tempted to take glory and honor upon ourselves for something we didn't do. In this session, Steve Ham shares the truths found in Psalm 127 which provide insight into this very issue.

Steve challenges us to be careful about being distracted from our calling, taking care to make sure that parenting our children is one of our top priorities. He also reminds us that we need to be grateful for our calling, seeing our children as blessings from the Lord rather than annoyances that interrupt our busy lives. Finally, Steve calls us to be committed to developing our children into "gospel warriors."

Objectives

At the end of this lesson, participants should be able to:

+ Articulate the biblical view that *every* child is a gift from the Lord.

+ Develop a plan to encourage their children to become "gospel warriors."

+ Describe the biblical teaching on God's sovereignty.

Getting Started

 Welcome participants to class, open in prayer, make announcements, etc.

In today's video, Steve Ham will be mining for us the truths found in Psalm 127. He likens the family to a fortress.

1. When you think of a "fortress," what comes to mind?

2. In what ways do you think your family could be a fortress?

The Family Fortress video outline

 Play *The Family Fortress* DVD.

Psalm 127:1–5

> Unless the LORD builds the house,
>   its builders labor in vain.
>   Unless the LORD watches over the city,
>   the watchmen stand guard in vain.
> In vain you rise early
>   and stay up late,
>   toiling for food to eat—
>   for he grants sleep to those he loves.
> Sons are a heritage from the LORD,
>   children a reward from him.
> Like arrows in the hands of a warrior
>   are sons born in one's youth.
> Blessed is the man
>   whose quiver is full of them.
>   They will not be put to shame
>   when they contend with their enemies in the gate. (NIV)

Verse 1: Parents rely on God for building and protecting family

Genesis 11:1–4

> Now the whole world had one language and a common speech. As men moved eastward, they found a plain in Shinar and settled there. They said to each other, "Come, let's make bricks and bake them thoroughly." They used

brick instead of stone, and tar for mortar. Then they said, "Come, let us build ourselves a city, with a tower that reaches to the heavens, so that we may make a name for ourselves and not be scattered over the face of the whole earth." (NIV)

Psalm 33:16–18

No king is saved by the size of his army; no warrior escapes by his great strength. A horse is a vain hope for deliverance; despite all its great strength it cannot save. But the eyes of the Lord are on those who fear him, on those whose hope is in his unfailing love. (NIV)

Verse 2: Parents are warned about the distraction of the world

1 Timothy 6:6

But godliness with contentment is great gain. (NIV)

Verse 3: Parents need to be grateful in their calling

Children are a gift from God

Verses 4–5: Parents are to be committed to the commission

Proverbs 27:11

Be wise, my son, and bring joy to my heart; then I can answer anyone who treats me with contempt. (NIV)

Family is a fortress and a lighthouse

Bringing It Home

 Use this time to discuss the following questions with participants. Many of the illustrations used in the video are available on the DVD for you to refer to as necessary.

1. This curriculum has focused on the responsibilities that the Lord has given to parents in training their children. Psalm 127:1 provides an important reminder that our responsibility must be understood in light of God's sovereignty. As we think about guiding our children into a love for the Lord and His Word, we need to keep in mind that *we* are ultimately not in control of the eternal destiny of our children. What do the following verses teach about salvation? Read Ephesians 1:3–4, Ephesians 2:8–10 and 2 Thessalonians 2:13.

2. One danger in studying what the Scripture says about parenting is that in our zeal to implement the practical principles, we neglect to cultivate our dependence upon the God who alone has the power to bless those principles and give us the strength to carry them out. We reduce child-training to determinism: "If I do A, B and C, my children will respond with X, Y and Z, with timing Q." Read John 15:1–8 and Psalm 33:16–22. How does Jesus in John 15:1–8 affirm what the psalmist teaches in Psalm 127:1?

3. One crucial way we express our dependence upon God is through prayer. We must be continually before the throne of God, interceding for our children's salvation and maturity, begging mercy for our many shortcomings as parents. How can we apply the following verses in how we pray for our children? Mark 11:22–24, Luke 11:5–10 and Colossians 4:2 (also 2 Chronicles 7:14; Psalm 5:1–3; Romans 12:12; Ephesians 6:18; Philippians 4:4–7; 1 Thessalonians 5:16–18).

4. How does James 1:5–8 apply to our prayers for our children?

5. Far too often, older parents (and fathers, in particular) claim the one thing they regret most is not having spent more time with their children. For whatever reason, parents can become distracted and fail to remember their God-given task of training and nurturing their children.

   What are some activities or events that can potentially distract you, keeping you from spending time with your family?

Of course, parents are not the only ones who can become distracted from their calling. Our children can also be distracted from their calling to love and serve Christ. What types of activities and opportunities can take priority over worshiping Christ? Are the activities that your children are currently involved in helping them to love God and His Word or are they distracting them from passionately serving the Lord Jesus Christ?

6. What do the following verses teach about the nature and origin of the unborn? Psalm 139:13–14 and Jeremiah 1:5

What are some ways you may have failed to see your children as blessings from the Lord?

How did your parents express their affection for you? How do you express your love for your children?

7. Sometimes discontent can creep into a parent's life. For example, some parents continually wish that their children were older so that they won't have to deal with "childishness" and can enjoy them more. Others can experience discontent on a more moment-by-moment basis. For example, "Only thirty more minutes until bath time and then the kids will be in bed, and I can spend time with my spouse or just relaxing."

Discuss some other ways that parents can exhibit discontent as they are raising their children. What are some steps you can take to guard against this?

8. Steve mentioned that we should be training our children to become "gospel warriors." One aspect of training our children in the nurture and admonition of the Lord is teaching and equipping them to fulfill the Great Commission (Matthew 28:19–20). In what ways can you raise children who are "missions-minded" and have a passion for evangelizing the lost?

 Watch *Putting It into Practice—Missions and your children*.

Of course, the primary way children learn the importance of reaching out to others is by watching their parents. How are you involved in sharing with and ministering to others? What are some ways that you can become more involved in your local church? What are some ways that you can minister in your community? (Perhaps volunteering at a soup kitchen or with a local boys and girls club, or conducting street evangelism.)

 Close in prayer, and briefly go over the homework assignment with participants.

Homework

1. During this week, read Proverbs 21–25 with your spouse (we suggest reading one chapter per day). In a journal, write down the insights that both of you glean from these chapters. Additionally, consider the following questions:

   • What do these proverbs teach about discipline?

   • What does Solomon teach about the nature of children in these verses?

   • How does Solomon communicate with his children in this passage?

   • Solomon frequently compares the behavior of the wise to the behavior of the foolish. What are the characteristics of the wise? What behaviors characterize the life of the foolish? Make a list of the characteristics of each as you go through this book. Is your life more characteristic of the wise or of the foolish? Because we can do nothing apart from the Lord, ask Him to show you areas in which you need to put off foolish behavior and put on the behavior of the wise. As you pray, ask Him to help you train your children to be wise. Most importantly, pray with an attitude of belief (read James 1:5–6).

2. One of the ways that some people excuse killing babies who are still in the womb is by claiming they are not really human. One of the justifications provided for this idea is the concept of "embryonic recapitulation" or "ontogeny recapitulates phylogeny." If you've ever heard this argument, visit AnswersInGenesis.org/go/embryonic to find out reasons why this isn't valid.

3. Sometimes we can get so carried away with carrying out the responsibilities the Lord has given us that we fail to remember the sovereignty of the Creator over His creation. Take some time this week to read and meditate on the following verses. What do these passages teach about God's sovereign control?

Exodus 8:22

Exodus 9:3–6

Exodus 10:21–23

Deuteronomy 8:18

1 Kings 17:2–4

Psalm 22:8

Psalm 33:11

Psalm 103:19

Psalm 115:3

Psalm 135:6

Psalm 147:15–18

Proverbs 16:4, 9

Proverbs 19:21

Proverbs 21:1, 30

Isaiah 14:27

Isaiah 40:17–18

Isaiah 46:9–10

Daniel 4:17, 35

Amos 4:7–10

Mark 4:39

John 3:27

Acts 17:28

Romans 9:15

Ephesians 1:3–5

1 Timothy 6:13–17

Hebrews 1:3

4. Following are some specific passages of Scripture that you might want to use as you pray for your children. As you look up these passages, write beside each something that you can pray for your children.

Ephesians 1:17–18

Ephesians 3:16–19

Philippians 1:9–11

Colossians 1:9–10

2 Thessalonians 1:11–12

5. Although men are to be the providers of their homes, many husbands and fathers rise early and retire late in order to spend more time at work, at the expense of spending time with their wife and children. If this is true of you, prayerfully consider how you can modify your schedule in such a way that honors and reflects the Lord's priorities for men. If you aren't around to guide your children, who will do it?

Fathers, what time concerns do you have that can prevent you from effectively leading and managing your family?

Mothers, what time concerns can keep you from concentrating on loving your husband and children?

6. As you read the following verses, make a note of those promises that you would like to spend time meditating on and memorizing:

Psalm 3:4–6

Proverbs 3:21–26

Isaiah 26:3

Matthew 6:24–34

1 Timothy 6:6–10

1 Peter 5:6–7

7. There are many tools that help you learn to effectively share the gospel with others. Some of these are listed in the "For More Information" section. Choose one or two to review with your family. If you haven't already, you may want to choose two or three missionaries to pray for regularly and correspond with as a family.

8. Continue working on drafting a family mission statement that will help you and your spouse to parent your children. What does the Creator want for your children? What verses can you use to guide you?

For More Information

+ *Fearfully and Wonderfully Made* (DVD)

"The question is not when does life begin, but when does a person begin?" Dr. David Menton explains from anatomical science and biology the truth of Psalm 139:13–16, which says that God weaves us together in the womb. This illustrated lecture also reveals the amazing and intricate design of the womb and the processes of fertilization, implantation, embryonic development and birth itself. Dr. Menton shows that each of these is a series of miracles (irreducible complexities) that cannot be explained by chance and random processes. Even more important, as Dr. Menton explains with grace and sensitivity in the wrap-up of the video, is the second "birth" process of salvation explained in John 3.

+ *George Mueller of Bristol: His Life of Prayer and Faith* by A.T. Pierson

George Mueller was living proof that God can be known intimately, that He is a faithful companion, and that prayer yields miraculous results. This classic biography tells of George Mueller's dependence on prayer and how his compassionate concern for orphans in Bristol, England shaped decades of missionary and social endeavors throughout the world.

+ *Why Won't They Listen?* by Ken Ham

This revolutionary book has already opened the eyes of thousands of Christians showing why the traditional methods of evangelism are not reaching today's humanistic, evolutionized culture. By applying proven soul-winning methods as found in the Scriptures, this book will revolutionize your witnessing.

- *Simple Tools for Brain Surgery* (DVD)

  Christians are sometimes intimidated by or even afraid to talk with many theists, new-agers and evolutionists. Too often, we fear we won't have answers to their tough questions. Now, you can learn how to engage people in conversation without fear. On this video you will learn—and actually put into practice—four killer questions that will help to destroy the secular thinking that is encasing the minds of friends, relatives and others.

- www.AnswersInGenesis.org/go/embryonic

- www.eeinternational.org (Evangelism Explosion website)

- www.wayofthemaster.com (Way of the Master website)

DEVELOPING A BIBLICAL MINDSET ABOUT MONEY AND POSSESSIONS

You will need DVD 5 for this lesson

Overview

In previous lessons we've discovered what the Bible teaches about various areas of parenting, including discipline and communication. In this session, our attention turns to the matter of finances—one area that many parents neglect to teach to their children. This may be because the parents themselves do not have a handle on biblical stewardship, or because they simply haven't thought much about it. And yet, the Bible is filled with warnings and exhortations about how we should manage our possessions.

In this session, we will be examing the foundational Scriptural principles concerning possessions so that, by God's grace, we can make wise decisions and train our children appropriately in this area.

Preparing for the Lesson

This is the fifth lesson in which the teaching section is led by you, the facilitator, rather than by video. Please spend time going over the material in this lesson during the week before you are scheduled to present this lesson.

- The illustrations and *Putting It into Practice* segments are available on DVD 5.

- If you, as the instructor, have any appropriate personal anecdotes that enhance or illustrate the points made in this lesson and honor the Lord, please feel free to add them as you go along.

- We have provided multiple Bible passages to read and study throughout these facilitator-led sessions. The verses in parentheses are supplemental to the primary verses and may be read as you have time (otherwise, encourage participants to read them during the following week).

- For the sake of time, you may want to write the passage references given throughout the lesson on individual slips of paper beforehand and pass them out to participants, asking them to read their assigned passage at the appropriate time. Or you may want to have everyone turn to the passage being discussed. The decision is left to you.

Objectives

At the end of this lesson, participants should be able to:

- Explain the Bible's teaching on the relationship between wisdom and wealth.

- Properly define Christian stewardship.

- Apply biblical priorities to financial decisions.

- Develop practical ideas for teaching children biblical principles of finances.

Getting Started

 Welcome participants to class, open in prayer, make announcements, etc.

This is *not* the most important session in this study.

How's that for an introduction? Our culture is infatuated with money, and Christendom is not particularly immune to this infatuation. When it comes to parenting, the Scripture emphasizes topics covered in prior sessions such as godly modeling and instruction, discipline and prayer. Our priorities should reflect the Scripture's priorities, and those foundations must be established before considering secondary issues such as finances.

Nonetheless, our attitude toward finances is important. It's been said that Jesus taught about money more than heaven, hell, prayer and faith. While this may be a bit overstated, one cannot miss how often our Messiah used teachings about money and possessions to communicate critical lessons. As parents, we also impart many practical life lessons to our children through finances—explicitly in our instruction, and implicitly as they observe how we handle our finances. Let's begin by contemplating the following questions.

How would you define Christian stewardship?

Have you thought about how you will teach your children about properly managing their finances?

Lesson

ILLUSTRATION 10-00

Let's begin the lesson with developing an understanding of the proper relationship between wisdom and wealth.

A. Understanding the proper relationship between wisdom and wealth

It's been observed that most drivers consider anyone they pass to be a slowpoke, but anyone who passes them to be a crazy driver. We live in a world framed in extremes, and Christian views on money are no exception. We are quick to judge those wealthier than we as lawless lovers of money, compromising wherever necessary to build their personal empires. However, if someone challenges our financial decisions, we may be quick to perceive him as a whistle-blowing, Bible-thumping sermonizer who is ignorant of any financial sense and who thinks all money is evil.

1. A question of priorities

ILLUSTRATION 10-01

Money itself is amoral; we can use it to support God's work or to oppose it. We must recognize that any conflict between wealth and biblical wisdom is a conflict of *priorities*. Repeatedly, the Scripture specifically extols wisdom as a more lofty pursuit than wealth. It does not teach that those who are wealthy are necessarily unwise or that those who are wise should be unwealthy.

 Read Proverbs 3:13–16 and 8:10–21 (Proverbs 16:16; 2 Chronicles 1:11–12)

What are some of the fruits of wisdom revealed in these verses?

> Answer:
>
> · Long life (Proverbs 3:16)
>
> · Honor (Proverbs 3:16, 8:18)
>
> · Riches (Proverbs 3:16, 8:18, 21)

- Leadership (Proverbs 8:15–16)

- Righteousness (Proverbs 8:18)

Note that Scripture does not dichotomize wealth and wisdom—some of the fruits of wisdom involve financial blessing. The question is one of *priorities*. Solomon was commended for choosing wisdom, and God chose to add the other blessings in turn (2 Chronicles 1:11–12).

Let's think about the priorities we are teaching our children. In what ways are we instilling in them a love for wisdom? In what ways are we instilling in them a love for wealth and possessions *over* a love for wisdom? Do our priorities reflect the Bible's?

Answer: Allow participants to respond and reflect.

 Read Matthew 6:19–24

Wealth becomes immoral when it becomes our master. We err when our decisions are not based on, "Is this in line with the ways of God's Kingdom?" This point is crucial:

> The path to good stewardship lies not through a forest of self-help secrets, ten easy steps or expert consultants, but along the straight and narrow path of scouring the Scripture and pleading to our Father for wisdom.

2. **The dangers of wealth taking priority**

 Read Proverbs 15:16–17, 19:1 and 22:1 (Proverbs 19:22, 28:6)

These proverbs imply that it may be necessary at times to forgo wealth to maintain high character. What negative characteristics that may be associated with riches are implied in these verses?

Answer:

- Household turmoil (Proverbs 15:6, 16)

- Hatred (Proverbs 15:17)

- Loss of integrity (Proverbs 19:1, 22, 28:6)

- Perverse speech (Proverbs 19:1)

- Suffering reputation (Proverbs 22:1)

B. What is Christian stewardship?

ILLUSTRATION 10-02

Every gift we have comes from God (James 1:17). The Scripture asserts not only that all things were created *by* God the Son, but *for* Him as well (Colossians 1:16–17).

It follows, then, that every Christian is a steward of God's resources. Our children, time, finances, house and every other gift are from the Lord, and are to be dedicated to His purposes.

One of the favorite expressions children use is, "It's mine!" How can we use these principles to teach our children about stewardship when we hear such exclamations?

Answer: Allow participants to respond.

1. **Stewardship is principally a matter of obedience**

    ILLUSTRATION 10-03

     Have someone read the following illustration:

    > Suppose you delegate to your five-year-old the responsibility of watering the family garden. After demonstrating the correct technique, you give specific instructions on each plant's watering needs. For several weeks, everything is going well as your child obediently waters each plant according to his father's instruction. However, your child notices that the pole beans just aren't coming up very fast, and he is anxious to enjoy their crop. So he decides (in the fullness of his five-year-old wisdom) that if a half-cup of water per week for each plant makes them grow at the rate he's been observing, how much faster would they grow with ten cups of water each week! His motives are pure—how proud his daddy will be when those beans come up so much faster so the family can enjoy them and even plant more! Of course, after a few weeks of such care, the plants' roots are completely submerged, killing the plants and eliminating any harvest.

    Although wanting to be a good steward and get the most out of the pole beans for the good of the family, your child did not follow your instructions, determining instead that he knew better than you how to care for the plants. Likewise, in the name of "good stewardship," we can sometimes go beyond God's commands to us regarding wisely handling our wealth.

    Now, our gardening analogy quickly breaks down because we parents, as fallen humans, are certainly capable of error, and it's not unreasonable that our children (especially as they grow in maturity) will have insights we have not considered. But our heavenly Father knows no such limitation. There will never be a time when we come up with an idea to which God slaps His forehead and says, "Man! Great idea! Why didn't *I* think of that?"

Read 1 Samuel 15:22

If we're honest, how often do we justify Scripturally-questionable actions in the name of "being a good steward"? We delude ourselves into thinking we are offering great sacrifices to God, when He would prefer simple obedience.

ILLUSTRATION 10-04

We offer, then, the following caution:

> Stewardship is not principally concerned with maximizing the return on God's resources, but above all with being faithfully obedient to God's commands about using those resources.

2. **Good stewardship often generates a positive tangible return**

   ILLUSTRATION 10-05

 Read Matthew 25:14–30

Often, good stewardship *does* result in decisions that produce tangible profits. The proverbs repeatedly make this connection, and the parable of the talents implies this relationship.

What was the result of the first two slaves' stewardship? For what were they praised?

> Answer: The result was that their master's money multiplied—a positive return. They are praised, however, not for the return, but for their faithfulness.

For what was the wicked slave condemned?

> Answer: The final servant is condemned—and this is especially important—not because he tried and failed to generate a positive return, but because he was disobedient (wicked and lazy).

3. **Good stewardship may demand "poor" (by the world's standards) financial decisions**

   ILLUSTRATION 10-06

 Read Luke 14:12–14 (Luke 6:27–36)

In this parable, the faithful steward will make what the world considers to be a foolish investment by inviting to his banquet only those who lack the means to repay. He looks forward to his repayment at the resurrection. In contrast, worldly business prowess motivates another to invite his friends, family and the rich, with sights on repayment in this life. The *inability* of the guests to repay is *precisely* what makes the former decision *good* stewardship; on the other hand, the *ability* of friends, family and the rich to repay is *precisely* what makes the latter decision *poor* stewardship.

4. **Learning from the widow's coins**

   ILLUSTRATION 10-07

   The resolution to this paradox lies in how we define success. Worldly success is defined by tangible financial and material returns, but the Kingdom's fruit includes intangibles such as righteousness, joy and peace, and is not so conveniently plotted and graphed.

    Read Mark 12:41–44

   We are tempted to read Jesus' statement, "this poor widow put in more than all the contributors to the treasury" (NASB), as mere hyperbole. Consider, however, that the vast sums that the wealthy put into the coffers have long since been spent, but the poor widow's generosity is still having an impact on the Kingdom as we read and reflect on her actions to this day. Truly, the widow's contribution, although smaller according to worldly measures, has had a greater return in Kingdom economy.

5. **Beware of pragmatism**

   ILLUSTRATION 10-08

   Tragically, just as the church has, by-and-large, accepted the world's wisdom on evolution and the age of the earth, some Christians are equally guilty of compromising biblical authority by accepting secular financial principles and allowing them to take precedence over the Scripture's principles of stewardship.

   Pragmatism is the philosophy that the success of a decision is based on that decision's observable practical results. If a particular decision generates more money, more "decisions" for Christ, a more positive response from others or more visible results, it is, to a pragmatist, good stewardship. On the contrary, if a decision fails to produce such tangibles, it is bad, and needs to be reevaluated. Just like Satan in Genesis 3, pragmatism tempts us to judge by appearance rather than the Word of God. (A more thorough critique of pragmatism is provided in some of the resources listed in the "For more information" section.)

   Friends, when we compromise Scriptural principles, the profits gained are completely irrelevant; we are guilty of adultery with the world (James 4:4).

   To review this section:

   > God is not depending on you as a parent to read dozens of books and listen to dozens of "experts" to uncover the secret keys of financial and time management in order to be a good steward. He is expecting you, however, to know His Word and be obedient to the principles therein.

C. Getting your children involved

 Watch *Putting It into Practice—Children and Finances*.

One man offered the following lessons he learned from his earthly father:

> Starting in sixth grade, I delivered newspapers from which I earned roughly $70 every other week. My dad insisted that I save a specified portion for the church, and save half of it. Still, when you are twelve years old and have no rent, food, or other bills, the remainder is A LOT of money! Nevertheless, I always managed to be short, and couldn't fathom where the money was going. (I often accused my siblings of stealing it....) My dad forced me to record every transaction so that I could look back on it later and understand what was happening. (Looking back, I am sure my father knew what was happening, but wanted me to discover it for myself.) You know what I found out? An immature young adult can spend a *lot* of money on video games, candy bars, video games, magazines, soda pop and video games.
>
> Now, even after this revelation, I can't say that I made wise decisions as an unregenerate self-absorbed pagan, but once the Lord did grant me repentance, I already had the tools to make informed financial decisions in accord with my new God-given priorities. Those priorities had already been taught to me by the instruction and example of my parents, even though I rebelled against them while living in slavery to sin.
>
> I might also mention that the forced paper route savings helped my wife and me avoid a lot of unnecessary debt when we were first starting out. That lesson, from my earthly father, has made a huge impact.

The point is this: You are the parent, and "foolishness is bound up in the heart of a child." Do not be afraid to *impose* on your children Bible-based standards of diligence, integrity, planning, contentment and other lessons of wisdom that can be taught from the financial realm. As often as appropriate, keep them informed on how you are making financial decisions and include them in the process. And pray, pray, pray for God's mercy to work deep within their hearts to be faithful stewards of the riches He will entrust to them some day.

Bringing It Home

Read Matthew 6:19–20. As with everything else, the goal of being a wise steward of what God has entrusted to us is to further the gospel of Christ with our time and money. As we go through the following verses, keep this principle in mind. How can we use what we have to fulfill the Great Commission? How can we teach this to our children?

For this part of the session, we'll be reading through categorized lists of verses covering specific topics such as finances, possessions and employment. As we read these verses, we'll be noting the principles expressed in each, and then we'll be discussing how we might apply them in our own lives and instill them into the hearts of our children.

> Note: This is by no means an exhaustive list. Encourage participants to write down additional verses they discover in their own studies. If you are doing this study in a group setting, you will undoubtedly be limited in time; the underlined verses will provide a good summary of those topics you are able to address. It will be most helpful to go through all the verses when you have the opportunity— encourage participants to do so, as well.

Before continuing, let's keep in mind a cautionary note. The principles in Scripture are black-and-white, but their application may not be. A decision that is excellent stewardship for one may be selfishly motivated for another. For example, paying forty dollars per month for high-speed internet to play online video games five hours per week while neglecting your family, is quite different than paying forty dollars per month for high-speed internet to enable you to work from home and spend five more hours per week with your family. We must take care not to justify foolish decisions and also to not self-righteously judge the decisions of others in the no-win game of spiritual one-upmanship. As believers, we have the Holy Spirit to guide us.

1. **The most important commands**

   Matthew 7:12   Matthew 22:37–40   Mark 12:28–34   Galatians 5:14

   Principles:

Application:

2. **Work and laziness**

Proverbs 6:6–11	Proverbs 10:4–5	Proverbs 10:26
Proverbs 12:11	Proverbs 12:24	Proverbs 12:27
Proverbs 13:4	Proverbs 13:11	Proverbs 14:4
Proverbs 14:23	Proverbs 15:19	Proverbs 18:9
Proverbs 19:15	Proverbs 19:24	Proverbs 20:4
Proverbs 20:13	Proverbs 21:5	Proverbs 21:25–26
Proverbs 22:13	Proverbs 23:21	Proverbs 24:30–34
Proverbs 26:13–16	Proverbs 28:19–20	Proverbs 30:7–9
Matthew 25:21	2 Thessalonians 3:6–12	Psalm 127:1–2

Principles:

Application:

3. **Debt**

Psalm 37:21–22   <u>Proverbs 22:7</u>

Principles:

Application:

4. **Giving**

Psalm 112:5	Proverbs 3:9–10	Proverbs 3:27–28
<u>Proverbs 11:24–26</u>	Proverbs 19:17	Proverbs 21:14
Proverbs 22:9, 16	Proverbs 28:27	Matthew 5:42
<u>Matthew 6:1–4</u>	Luke 12:32–34	Philippians 4:10–20
1 Corinthians 16:1–2	2 Corinthians 8–9	<u>1 John 3:16–17</u>

Principles:

Application:

5. **Contentment / indulgent living**

<u>Proverbs 21:17</u>	Proverbs 23:21	Proverbs 30:7–9
Philippians 4:10–19	<u>1 Timothy 6:6–8</u>	Hebrews 13:5

   Principles:

   Application:

6. **Surety / countersigning on another's loan**

Proverbs 6:1–5	Proverbs 11:15	<u>Proverbs 17:18</u>
Proverbs 20:16	Proverbs 22:26–27	

   Principles:

Application:

7. **Integrity**

Proverbs 10:2	Proverbs 11:1	Proverbs 11:18
Proverbs 12:22	Proverbs 13:11	Proverbs 13:18
Proverbs 15:27	Proverbs 16:8	Proverbs 16:11
Proverbs 19:1	Proverbs 20:10	Proverbs 20:17
Proverbs 20:23	Proverbs 21:6	Proverbs 22:1
Proverbs 28:6	Proverbs 28:8	Amos 8:4–7

Principles:

Application:

8. **Persuasion and marketing**

Proverbs 16:21	Proverbs 16:23	Proverbs 27:2
Proverbs 28:21	Matthew 7:12	Mark 9:42
2 Corinthians 9:7	Philippians 2:3–8	James 2:1–9
2 Peter 2:18		

Principles:

Application:

9. Priorities: loving God or loving money

Ecclesiastes 5:10–11	Proverbs 15:16–17	Proverbs 17:24
Proverbs 20:15	Proverbs 21:3	Proverbs 22:4
Proverbs 23:4–5	Proverbs 24:3–6	Matthew 6:19–34
Matthew 16:24–26	Luke 6:27–36	1 Timothy 6:10
Hebrews 13:5		

Principles:

Application:

10. Dependence on the Lord

<u>Deuteronomy 8:17–18</u>	Proverbs 11:28	Proverbs 13:11
Proverbs 16:1–3	Proverbs 16:9	<u>Proverbs 18:11</u>
Proverbs 23:4–5	Luke 12:13–34	<u>1 Timothy 6:17–19</u>
James 4:13–16	James 5:1–6	

Principles:

Application:

11. Saving / Presumption

<u>Proverbs 21:20</u>	Proverbs 13:22	Psalm 19:13
Matthew 4:5–7		

Principles:

Application:

12. Taxes

Matthew 22:15–22   Romans 13:1–10

Principles:

Application:

 Close in prayer, and briefly go over the homework assignment with participants.

Homework

What follows is a practical plan for implementing some of the ideas expressed in this lesson. Over the next week, go through these items and think about how you can implement them into your life and the life of your family. Consider spending a few weeks discussing biblical principles of stewardship with your children during your family devotion time.

Study

Read and prayerfully meditate on the verses in this session, including the ones you did not have time to consider during the class. Supplement them with any others you come across in your studies. As you go along, discuss these with your spouse and write down your conclusions and ways you might apply those principles in your family's life.

Summarize and set specific goals

Review your conclusions and, with input from your spouse, write down specific goals and priorities on how you want to use your money and other possessions. For example, you might determine to begin paying off any credit card debt you have, to begin supporting a missionary, to save more or to provide for your local food bank.

Create a budget

It is wise to keep abreast of your resources (Proverbs 27:23–24). Many people find a written budget an extremely helpful tool for planning and accountability. At its most basic level, setting up a budget involves noting all income sources, setting limits on expense categories and implementing a system (e.g., envelopes, spreadsheets, financial software) to keep track of your progress. The resources at the end of this lesson contain helpful tips on establishing and sticking to a budget. You and your spouse both need to commit to following what you've decided on.

Create a schedule

Although this lesson focuses primarily on finances, many of the concepts can be applied to our attitude and the stewardship of our time. By carefully planning the 24 hours you have been given each day, you may find yourself accomplishing much more that is worthwhile. Discuss with your spouse some ways that both of you can become better stewards of your time and how you can better manage your children's time.

Cultivate dependence on the Lord and guidance by the Spirit

Keep ever at the front of your mind that "The mind of man plans his way, But the LORD directs his steps" (Proverbs 16:9, NASB). Pray earnestly for wisdom and mercy.

For More Information

+ *Master Your Money* (book and workbook) by Ron Blue

Contains helpful tips on setting up a budget, investment strategies and long-term planning.

+ *Does the Truth Matter Anymore?* DVD series by John MacArthur

  Provides a detailed critique of the error of pragmatism and felt-needs philosophy. It is particularly focused on the marketing-driven church error, but is also relevant to personal finances and business decisions.

+ *The Christian and His Finances* audio tape by John MacArthur

  Provides a good introduction to the proper Christian mindset concerning finances.

+ *Managers of Their Homes* by Steve and Teri Maxwell

  Contains helpful tips for daily scheduling for homeschooling families. Available from Titus2.com.

+ www.Crown.org (Crown Financial Ministries website)

PARENTING PRACTICES

You will need DVD 5 for this lesson

Overview

In this final session, Steve Ham reminds us of three areas that we've spent time going over in the past weeks: submission, discipline and nurturing our children with Scripture. He challenges parents to consider the evangelistic mission that they have toward their children and reminds us that God has no grandchildren. He ends with the challenge: "What biblical legacy will you leave for your children?"

Objectives

At the end of this lesson, participants should be able to:

+ Define the parents' responsibility in sharing the gospel with their children.

+ Describe what the gospel is.

+ Describe some examples of how to refrain from provoking their children to wrath.

Getting Started

 Welcome participants to class, open in prayer, make announcements, etc.

This is the final session of this course. In the video, Steve Ham will be reviewing many of the concepts that we've discussed over the past weeks. First, however, let's consider the following question.

Do you agree or disagree with the statement "God has no grandchildren"?

Parenting Practices video outline

 Play *Parenting Practices* DVD.

Our post-modern world

Romans 1:18–32

> Hearts have been darkened

> Willing, lawless rebellion

> God has given them over to wickedness

> One attribute: disobedience to parents

Ephesians 6:1–4

> Children, obey your parents in the Lord, for this is right."Honor your father and mother" which is the first commandment with a promise—"that it may go well with you and that you may enjoy long life on the earth." Fathers, do not exasperate your children; instead, bring them up in the training and instruction of the Lord. (NIV)

Deuteronomy 5:16

> Honor your father and your mother, as the Lord your God has commanded you, so that you may live long and that it may go well with you in the land the Lord your God is giving you. (NIV)

The Submission command

> "Does that mean that, if I am a dutiful son or daughter, I am of necessity going to live to great age? No, that does not follow. But the promise certainly means this, that if you want to live a blessed life, a full life under the benediction of God, observe this commandment. He may choose to keep you for a long time on this earth as an example and illustration. But however old you may be when you leave this world, you will know that you are under the blessing, and the good hand, of God." Dr. Martyn Lloyd-Jones, *Life in the Spirit: in Marriage, Home & Work*, 1973, page 246.

The Discipline command

> Proverbs 13:24

> > He who spares the rod hates his son, but he who loves him is careful to discipline him. (NIV)

> Do not tolerate dishonor

In what context is discipline necessary?

Do not exasperate children

Be Spirit-filled, not out of control

Ephesians 5:18

Don't get drunk on wine, which leads to debauchery. Instead be filled with the Spirit. (NIV)

Galatians 5:22–23

But the fruit of the Spirit is love, joy, peace, patience, kindness, goodness, faithfulness, gentleness and self-control. (NIV)

Be consistent

Don't discipline out of anger or loss of control

The Nutrition command

Matthew 3:7–10

But when he saw many of the Pharisees and Sadducees coming to where he was baptizing, he said to them: "You brood of vipers! Who warned you to flee from the coming wrath? Produce fruit in keeping with repentance. And do not think you can say to yourselves, 'We have Abraham as our father.' I tell you that out of these stones God can raise up children for Abraham. The ax is already at the root of the trees, and every tree that does not produce good fruit will be cut down and thrown into the fire. (NIV)

We have an evangelistic mission to our children

Galatians 6:14

May I never boast except in the cross of our Lord Jesus Christ, through which the world has been crucified to me, and I to the world. (NIV)

What biblical legacy will you leave for your children?

Bringing It Home

 Use this time to discuss the following questions with participants. Many of the illustrations used in the video are available on the DVD for you to refer to as necessary.

1. Throughout this course, we've been discussing the need to leave a legacy for our family that honors God and His Word. And yet, as Steve pointed out in this session, *God has no grandchildren.* John the Baptist made this truth brutally clear

in his rebuke of the Pharisees and Sadducees. Read Matthew 3:7–10. What misunderstanding did the Jews whom John addressed have?

Many people today are trusting in their family heritage for their salvation. We need to take care that we do not trust in this or any other thing apart from the saving grace of God to save us and our children. We can't just assume that because *we* have a personal relationship with the Creator that our children will also.

We already discussed the sovereignty of God in relation to salvation, but the Bible is also clear that *we* have a responsibility to share the gospel with our children. Read Acts 20:18–27; 1 Corinthians 9:19–22; 1 Corinthians 7:16 and Ezekiel 33:1–9. What do these passages teach about *our* responsibility?

What *is* the good news that we are to share with our children?

2. As Steve mentioned in this session, the Bible warns against provoking our children to wrath (Ephesians 6:4). What are some ways you've noticed that you might provoke your children to wrath? What are some steps that you can take to prevent doing this in the future?

Watch _Putting It into Practice—Provoking children_.

3. Steve also discussed the need for us to give our children truthful nutrition. Let's think for a moment about what we are "feeding" to our children. What are some things that we use to "nourish" our children?

Are these things truly nourishing our children, or are they actually influencing our children to "understand the whole of reality without God" (as Ken mentioned earlier)?

 Watch *Putting It into Practice—Media Monitoring.*

Obviously there is no "thou shalt not watch television" command given in the Bible, but media can play a major role in shaping how our children view the world, if we allow it to. Evaluate what you are "feeding" to your children—books, videos, television programs. What changes can you make in what you are exposing your children to in order to achieve the goals you have set for your children?

4. As we bring this study to a close, we need to remember that in order to leave a legacy of godliness to our children, we ourselves need to be growing in the grace and knowledge of our Lord and Savior Jesus Christ (2 Peter 3:18). We cannot, in our own strength, raise our children as the Lord desires us to. As Steve exhorted us in this lesson, we need to be constantly depending on the Holy Spirit to work in us and through us, as He continually conforms us to the image of God's dear Son. Read Galatians 5:16–26. Is your life more reflective of one who gratifies the desires of the sinful nature or of one who lives by the Spirit? Consider carefully the example that you are setting for your children as you teach them in both words and actions.

5. Over the past weeks, you have been developing a mission statement to help guide you in parenting your children. Share your mission statement with the class. With your spouse, commit to implement your mission statement in your parenting.

 Close in prayer, and briefly go over the homework assignment with participants.

Homework

1. During this week, read Proverbs 26–31 with your spouse (we suggest reading one chapter per day). In a journal, write down the insights that both of you glean from these chapters. Additionally, consider the following questions:

   + What do these proverbs teach about discipline?

   + What do Solomon, Agur and King Lemuel teach about the nature of children in these passages?

   + These men frequently compare the behavior of the wise to the behavior of the foolish. What are the characteristics of the wise? What behaviors characterize the life of the foolish? Make a list of the characteristics of each as you go through this book. Is your life more characteristic of the wise or of the foolish? Because we can do nothing apart from the Lord, ask Him to show you areas in which you need to put off foolish behavior and put on the behavior of the wise. As you pray, ask Him to help you train your children to be wise. Most importantly, pray with an attitude of belief (read James 1:5–6).

2. This week, have each family member keep a log of the time he or she spends in front of "screens" (television, computer, hand-held games, etc.) What activities can you do to replace time spent in front of screens? Talk with your spouse about any changes that you believe might be necessary concerning the media that you allow your children to watch or read.

For More Information

+ *How to Get the Best Out of TV (Before It Gets the Best Out of You)* by Dale and Karen Mason

   Although now out of print, this book is available on many used book sites.

   In a style that combines humor with insight and practicality, authors Dale and Karen Mason first present a wake-up call to parents, and then equip them with a treasure chest of tools that help viewers get the best out of TV, without being battered by the bad!

   This "TV survival kit" features humorous and eye-opening stories plus statistics on TV viewing, video usage, etc. Includes little-known facts of how TV affects (and can actually enhance!) family communication and spiritual growth. You'll love the Masons' 10 proven ideas of how to reduce and/or improve TV-time, and their helpful reproducible forms which "jump start" your journey to better media management.

ANSWER KEY

Session 1: Getting Started

1. Allow participants to respond.

2. Allow participants to respond.

3. Allow participants to voice the legacy they believe they are leaving for their children. Throughout this series, we'll be challenging parents to reexamine and redefine their legacy, conforming it to what the Bible teaches parents should strive for.

4. Allow participants to respond. Later in this lesson, we'll be helping participants to develop biblically-derived goals for their children—goals that are Christ-centered rather than worldly.

Session 1: Bringing It Home

1. Allow for individual responses. Participants should be challenged to evaluate where they are spending their time and money.

    Allow for individual responses. Participants should develop ways that they can advance the kingdom of heaven within their own family.

2. Allow participants to think about their answer to this question. There's no need for them to answer this out loud, unless they want to discuss this question. Although most people will never be the prolific writers that Martin Luther or John Bunyan were, we never know how the Lord will use our children. We all need to endeavor to leave a spiritual legacy for our children and those within our sphere of influence.

3. He wants us to be completely committed to Him—to fear Him, walk in His ways, love Him, serve Him with our whole being.

    Allow participants to describe the legacy they would like to leave for their children. They should begin to see that the most important legacy they can leave for their children is a love for God and His Word. Throughout this course, we'll be examining practical ways that we can instill this love for the Creator in the hearts of our children.

4. Allow participants to voice their reasons for having and raising children, and their mission statement (if they have one). Throughout this lesson series, we'll be challenging parents to reexamine and redefine their goals

in raising their children, and we'll be helping them to develop a mission statement that is based on what the Bible teaches about childrearing.

5. Possible responses could include accounts about the "big bang," a discovery of a "missing link," new findings that the earth is billions of years old.

    1. Ask: How do they know this?

    2. Make sure we've correctly read the biblical passage that seems to be in conflict with the news report.

    3. If it seems worth your time, search for ways to counter what was heard.

    4. If no answers are currently available, wait and exercise faith—only God knows everything.

Session 2: Getting Started

1. Allow participants to respond. Don't expect participants to provide a detailed answer at this point—the video will help participants to formulate a response.

2. Allow participants to respond. Hopefully this lesson will address most, if not all, of the questions raised at this time. If not, please encourage participants to visit the "Get Answers" page at www.AnswersInGenesis.org/go/qa for more information on their particular questions.

Session 2: Bringing It Home

1. Each one of us! The Bible is clear that we have all sinned against a holy God and are deserving of eternal separation from Him.

2. God has decreed that the punishment for disobedience to His commands is death (Genesis 2:15–17; Romans 6:23). And yet, He graciously enables us to continue breathing (Acts 17:28), allowing us more opportunities to turn to Him in obedience.

3. Hopefully participants are now able to explain that death and suffering are not God's fault, but rather the result of our sin. God's original creation was perfect—cats were not originally created as killers. But Adam's disobedience changed the creation. Paul, in Romans 8:18–22, testifies that all of creation is suffering from the curse God placed on His creation as a result of Adam's sin. Animals which were originally vegetarian now have carnivorous tendencies. But, in the midst of this reminder that we live in a corrupted world, we need to remember that God has provided salvation for those who repent of their sins and by faith believe in the atoning sacrifice of Christ on the cross. For more information, see www.AnswersInGenesis.org/go/curse.

4. We can provide answers to the questions that people have concerning the Bible: Who was Cain's wife? Isn't evolution a fact? Don't fossils take millions of years to form? Haven't various methods proven the earth to be billions of years old? We can show them how true science confirms the Bible's teachings.

    We can explain specific problems with evolutionary ideas and the assumptions that go into the various age-dating methods. We can show how actual scientific findings have undermined the age-dating methods.

5. The Bible's moral teachings (including those about training children to be godly) have their foundation in the Bible's historical teachings. If the history isn't true, why should the moral teachings (e.g., about childrearing,

salvation) have any value? However, God as the Creator has laid down for His precious—but corrupted—creation rules for living our lives. These include commands about living lives that please Him and commands about raising our children. Because He is the authority, we must accept what He says as authoritative in all areas of our lives—we are not free to pick and choose the teachings we accept or reject.

6. It's important that we not run from such situations, but that we carefully explain to our children the answer from Scripture and science, showing them that the Bible can be trusted. In these cases, we could say that God created birds on Day 5 of the first week and dinosaurs on Day 6. Therefore, birds could not have evolved from dinosaurs, as birds were created one day before the land creatures! Scientifically, we could point out the ways in which bird feathers are structurally and biochemically different from reptilian scales and address the differences between the avian lung and the reptilian lung. See www.AnswersInGenesis.org/go/bird-evolution for more information. If they can't explain a biblically-based answer to their children when they encounter such a situation, then parents might want to write down the statement in question and let their children know that they'll be researching the answer once they return home, or once they're finished watching the movie.

Session 3: Getting Started

1. Allow participants to respond. During the video, Ken will be challenging the participants to consider carefully their choice of education for their children based on what the Bible teaches, and we'll discuss this topic in more detail after the video.

Session 3: Bringing It Home

1. Encourage participants to really examine the educational choice they've made in light of what the Bible teaches about the responsibility parents bear in "filling their children with salt." Is the educational situation they've put their children in truly one that will cultivate a hunger and desire to know the Lord? Is it helping their children to become more Christ-like? Is their choice based on "that's the way I was raised and look how I turned out"? Is it because they want to take the path of least resistance or because they're concerned about what their family and friends will think? Is it because they haven't considered other options?

    Educating children at home or in a Christian school may not be possible for everyone; however, the choices made should be well thought-out and based on what they believe the Lord is leading them to do, and not merely because "that's the way we've always done it." For those who are financially (or for other reasons) unable to homeschool or Christian school their children, discuss some ways that they can become more active in their children's education so that they are able to combat the wordly teaching their children are receiving.

    Parents who claim that a Christian school would "cost too much" might be challenged to consider some areas in which they may need to modify their spending or budgeting habits.

    Encourage parents to pray about their decision, seeking the Lord's face and His guidance and direction, taking care to make sure that whatever they decide is for the glory of the Lord.

2. The Word of God makes us wise for salvation; it is profitable for teaching, reproving, correcting, training in righteousness; it shows us what the Lord expects from us; it helps us to help others become more Christ-like. NOTE: We will be discussing *how* to use Scripture when training our children in session 7. For now, we

will focus on the importance of memorizing Scripture and practical ways that we can help our children to memorize the Word of God.

3. They will spend eternity either with Christ or suffering the wrath of God.

Session 4: Getting Started

Allow participants to discuss their responses.

Session 4: Bringing It Home

1. Yes, it matters. God has given each gender certain responsibilities that they are to fulfill within the family. When we disregard these commands, we are being disobedient to the Creator, and thus we are sinning. We are not being the examples to our children that we should be, and we are not showing them the importance of submitting ourselves to God's authority. How can we expect to teach them to be obedient when we, as parents, are not being obedient?

2. Allow participants to offer suggestions. These might include how to spend an evening; where and when to go out to eat; husbands helping out in the kitchen or with the kids without being asked; etc.

3. Allow participants to offer suggestions. These might include setting time aside each day to instruct your family; conversing more with your wife about what she is learning from the Scriptures; etc.

Session 5: Getting Started

The parents are allowing the children to make the decisions. Neither parents or children are filling their biblically prescribed roles.

Session 5: Bringing It Home

Allow paticipants to respond for each of these questions.

Session 6: Getting Started

1. Allow participants to respond. There may be both positive and negative connotations based on their personal experience and exposure to popular opinion.

2. Allow participants to discuss how they've handled their children's disobedience this past week.

Session 6: Bringing It Home

1. Proverbs 13:24 is especially helpful. Biblically, love motivates discipline, while withholding the rod is an act of hatred. This response looks long-term to the fruit produced by consistent discipline.

2. The primary difference is in the motivation. Discipline seeks to benefit the child; abuse seeks to harm the child. Discipline is done calmly and deliberately; abuse is done in anger and in retaliation. Also, abuse causes physical and emotional scars.

3. Children don't know what is expected of them. For example, if a child is not disciplined one day for talking back, and yet the next day, we get angry and say, "Don't speak to me like that!" and administer discipline, the child can become confused about which attitudes and behaviors are acceptable and which are not. Sinful behavior is always wrong, and we need to be careful to be consistent in correcting it, even when we're tired or simply "don't feel like it."

   When we are inconsistent with discipline, our children may try to "get away with" a behavior, perhaps thinking "maybe I won't be disciplined this time." We aren't training them according to God's standard, and they may begin to see discipline as a hit-or-miss process. We are teaching them that our words don't matter and that they don't always need to submit to our authority.

   Some ideas include: work together with your spouse, agreeing on which behaviors and attitudes are acceptable and which are not. Commit to disciplining your child at the time of the first offense, whether or not you feel like doing it.

4. Communicate your desire with your spouse and agree to keep each other accountable. If you are alone at the time, you may need to send the child to his room for a few minutes while you pray and ask the Lord to help change your attitude. Once you've calmed down, begin the discipline process.

5. The rod is God's ordained means of disciplining our children. First, verify that you are applying the rod correctly, and not provoking your child in another way. Make sure you are not neglecting your other responsibilities as a parent—modeling godly character and praying fervently on behalf of your children, for example. Also, ask yourself, "Have I been consistent in disciplining my children?" If your conscience is clear, be persistent and endure. Remember, the timing of when you might see fruit in your child's life is not guaranteed in Scripture. A child whose strong will resists correction might mature into an adult whose strong will resists being carried about by every wind of doctrine.

Session 7: Getting Started

1. Allow participants to respond.

2. One defines the problem using biblical terminology (1 Timothy 3:13; Titus 1:7); the other defends it as a normal (and thus excusable) behavior.

Session 7: Bringing It Home

1. Encourage participants to come up with a situation in which children whine.

   Most likely, depending on the situation, you are dealing with complaining (grumbling).

   Perhaps Philippians 2:14; Ephesians 4:29; Proverbs 25:28; 1 Thessalonians 5:16–18. Remember to also consider the "putting on" attribute, such as gratitude or respect.

Allow participants to come up with their own wording. Perhaps something like "Stephen, God says that we are to do all things without complaining." (Read with him or to him Philippians 2:14). "Do you think your attitude right now is pleasing to God?" (Read 1 Thessalonians 5:16–18) "God wants us to be joyful and give thanks in all situations. Why do you think you're having a hard time being joyful and giving thanks in this situation?" (Spend some time discussing why he's complaining—perhaps he isn't considering the goodness of God in giving us good gifts. Administer biblical discipline.) "Let's ask the Lord to help you to be joyful and willing to obey." (Pray.) "How can you re-say what you've just said to reflect an attitude that pleases God?"

2. Biblical: Use a calm, normal tone of voice. Ask, "Did you do as I asked?" Follow with a Bible-based discipline session.

   Unbiblical: Yell; use sarcasm; compare him with his sister who cleaned her room, count to 10; give him "just one more chance."

3. Biblical: You are respectful and humble; you make sure you have all the information; you base your conviction on Scripture; you determine to discuss it directly with the other party.

   Unbiblical: You use sarcasm, are proud, have a "thank-you-that-I'm-not-like-that-tax-collector" attitude; you slander another person or gossip about them.

4. Allow participants to respond.

5.

Behavior	Biblical characteristic to "put off"	Biblical characteristic to "put on"	Relevant verses
Fights with a sibling over a toy	Selfishness	Counting others more important than self	Philippians 2:3–4; Proverbs 11:24–25; Romans 12:20–21; James 3:13–18; 1 Peter 4:9–11
Refuses to take a bath	Stubborn; insubordinate	Respectful; obedient; submissive	Proverbs 8:13,15:32, 29:1; Ephesians 6:1–3; Philippians 2:1–11; Colossians 3:20; James 4:6; 1 Peter 5:5–6
Room is constantly messy	Laziness, sluggardness, slothfulness	Diligence	Proverbs 6:6–11, 10:4, 12:27, 14:23, 19:15, 26:13–16; Ecclesiastes 10:18; 1 Corinthians 10:31; 2 Thessalonians 3:13
Cries when you turn out the lights	Worry, anxiety	Trust	Proverbs 12:25; Matthew 6:25–34; Luke 12:22–30; Philippians 4:6–8
Consistently fails to say "thank you"	Ungratefulness	Gratitude; thanksgiving	Psalm 100; Matthew 14:19, 15:36, 26:26; Romans 1:20–22, 14:6–7; Colossians 3:15–17; 1 Thessalonians 5:17–18; 2 Timothy 3:1–5
Makes fun of a sibling when that sibling fails	Unkindness	Kindness; encouragement	Proverbs 11:17, 14:21–22, 19:17; Luke 6:35–36; 1 Corinthians 13:4; 2 Timothy 2:24; Titus 2:5
Does not ever want to stop playing video games	Idolatry	Loving God; loving neighbor as self	John 12:42–43; Proverbs 21:17, 29:25; Matthew 6:24, 20:26–28; Luke 9:23–24; 1 Corinthians 10:24, 13:5; Galatians 1:10, 5:19–21; Colossians 3:5–6; 1 Timothy 6:10; 2 Timothy 3:1–5; James 4:1; 1 John 5:21
Consistently provokes a sibling	Quarreling, fighting	Peace-making	Proverbs 13:10, 15:18, 17:14, 19, 20:3, Philippians 2:1–11; 2 Timothy 2:27; James 4:1–3
Constantly requests something new to do	Impatience; discontent	Patience; contentment	Proverbs 19:11, 25:15; Ecclesiastes 7:8; 1 Corinthians 13:4, 7; 2 Corinthians 6:4–9; Galatians 5:22; Colossians 3:12; James 1:2–4, 5:6–8

Session 8: Getting Started

Allow participants to respond.

Session 8: Bringing It Home

1.

Deuteronomy 6:4–6	The commands of God are to be upon our hearts and are to be what we teach to our children.
Deuteronomy 17:18–20	The king is to be guided by the commands of God.
Job 23:12	The words of the Lord were more important to Job than bread.
Psalm 12:6	The words of the Lord are pure, flawless, holy, separate from sin—in contrast to the words of men who are corrupted by sin.
Psalm 19:7–11	The Word of God revives the soul, gives wisdom, gives joy to the heart, provides direction. Compare this to the thoughts and opinions of men—can any man truly do these things?
Jeremiah 15:16	The words of the Lord are to be our joy and our heart's delight—we are not to derive our joy from temporary things.
Micah 2:7	The words of God do good to the upright.
Matthew 4:1–11	The Lord Jesus used the Word of God to refute Satan's temptations—not the words of men.
Mark 12:24	Jesus rebuked the Sadducees because they did not know the Scriptures or the power of God.
Luke 11:28	Those who hear the Word of God and obey it are blessed.
Luke 16:19–31	The Word of God is superior to miracles in converting the soul.
John 17:17	Sanctification (the process of being made holy) comes through the Word of God—not through the words of men.
Acts 20:32	The Word of God builds us up.
1 Corinthians 2:6–16	Paul spoke to the church at Corinth not with the wisdom of the age, but with the wisdom of God.
2 Corinthians 3:5	God is sufficient—we are not.
2 Corinthians 9:8–10	God supplies everything we need to do good.
Colossians 2:3–10	We are not to be captive to human tradition and worldly wisdom; we are to be rooted and grounded in Christ, and we have been given fullness in Christ.
Colossians 3:16	We are to use the word of Christ to teach and admonish others—not the words of psychologists, self-help gurus or the like.
1 Thessalonians 2:11–13	Paul urged the Corinthians to live godly lives with the Word of God, not the word of men.
2 Timothy 3:15–17	The Scriptures make us wise for salvation through faith in Christ. All Scripture is useful for teaching, rebuking, correcting and training in righteousness so that we are completely able to do every good work.
1 Peter 2:2–3	We are to crave the Word of God so that we can grow spiritually—not to be taken in and discipled by the words of men.

2 Peter 1:1–9	We have been given everything we need for life and godliness through the knowledge of Christ, which has been revealed to us in the Word of God.
1 John 2:20–27	The Holy Spirit instructs us about the Word of God.
Revelation 22:18–19	We are not to add to or take away from the God-breathed words in the Bible.

2. The Christians in Berea diligently searched the Scriptures to see if what Paul said was true.

3. Some examples might include reasoning away the resurrection of Christ by saying that He only fainted, or that His disciples stole His body from the tomb, based on the "fact" that dead men don't rise from the dead. Or explaining away the Virginal Conception of Christ by claiming that Mary wasn't really a virgin, based on the "fact" that virgins don't give birth to children. Or explaining away all the miracles in the Bible by developing "natural" explanations for them.

   There are several ways to respond to these claims. You may want to print some of the articles found at www.AnswersInGenesis.org/go/Jesus-Christ for participants to read, or direct them toward this site for more information.

4. Allow participants to respond.

5. Allow participants to respond.

Session 9: Getting Started

1. Allow participants to respond.

2. Allow participants to respond.

Session 9: Bringing It Home

1. Salvation is a work of God. The elect have been chosen before the foundation of the world. We are saved by grace through faith; our works do not contribute.

2. We cannot expect to bear fruit in our child training apart from our communion with Christ. Our toil will be in vain apart from the Lord's work.

3. We are commanded to be persistent in our prayers, praying in faith even when we do not see results like we expected. We are to pray believing that we have received what we have asked for. Certainly, this truth has been abused, particularly within the Word-faith movement, reducing God to a cosmic genie, obligated to fulfill our every selfish desire. But let us not throw out the baby with the bathwater; pray in faith that God is able to work mighty things in the hearts of your children, all to His glory.

4. We need to be asking the Lord for wisdom and guidance as we raise our children.

5. Allow participants to respond. Sometimes hobbies or sports activites can take priority over our family.

   Many Christians can tend to overemphasize "good" things (sports, jobs, hobbies, clubs, social activities, etc.) that are often good opportunities in themselves, but distort priorities and rob us of the passion to serve Christ. Parents who wouldn't dream of allowing their children to dishonor Christ in any overt way will allow their children to treat activities with such priority that service to, and worship of, Christ is neglected. Exhort participants to evaluate what they are encouraging their children to spend their time on—are they pursuing Christ, or are they pursuing other things?

6. Every child conceived in the womb is a precious gift from the Lord to the parents. We bear an awesome responsibility as stewards of these gifts.

   Allow participants to respond. Too often, parents can have a skewed view of their children—perhaps viewing their children as "mistakes," interruptions in their career plans, the focus of their world, etc.

   Allow participants to respond.

7. Allow participants to respond.

8. Allow participants to respond.

Session 10: Getting Started

Most Christians, when asked, have a pretty good working definition of stewardship: something along the lines of "using God's resources wisely." Later we will attempt to correct a subtle error we often commit when practically applying that definition.

Allow participants to respond.

Session 10: Bringing It Home

This is by no means an exhaustive list. Encourage participants to write down additional verses they discover in their own studies. If you are doing this study in a group setting, you will undoubtedly be limited in time; the underlined verses will provide a good summary of those topics you are able to address. It will be most helpful to go through all the verses when you have the opportunity—encourage participants to do so, as well.

1. **The most important commands**

   If we make our everyday decisions according to these commands, we are well on our way to biblical stewardship.

   In particular, the "golden rule" in Matthew 7:12 can be applied in situations not directly addressed in Scripture. Put yourself in the position of the affected party and ask, "If I were in his position, what decision would I want to be made?" Cultivate this attitude in your children, particularly as they relate to their siblings.

   We must not only consider the return on the decision, but what else could be done with that resource (money, time) if we made a different decision. Economists call this the "opportunity cost." We might argue that there's nothing wrong with spending an hour a day playing video games, but we must consider what is *not* being done with that hour. Have you communed with your Lord sufficiently today? Are you neglecting your spouse and children?

2. **Work and laziness**

   God has designed work as a means by which we can generate wealth. Our attitude should be eagerness to be involved in gainful employment, and thankful for that opportunity. Laziness is to be avoided at all costs, as is a get-rich-quick mentality. We can teach our children these principles early on by assigning chores, for example. Psalm 127:1-2 gives a balance; however, working overtime to impress the boss or get a bonus at the expense of neglecting your family is futility.

3. **Debt**

   A Christian is obligated to pay his debts. The Scripture presents debt as a very unwise thing in that it enslaves us to the lender.

4. **Giving**

   The Old and New Testaments unmistakably teach that a mark of a redeemed and faithful life is generosity. Give as you are led by the Spirit, not under compulsion (2 Corinthians 8-9); give secretly (Matthew 6); give to legitimate needs (Proverbs 22:16). In at least one circumstance, Paul encourages systematic giving based on God's blessing (1 Corinthians 16:1-2). You might provide your children an allowance as a means for them to practice and demonstrate generosity.

   Jesus showed us the greatest generosity in giving up glory to live with us and die for us. Our generosity should reflect Christ as we give to enable others to hear about the gospel.

5. **Contentment / indulgent living**

   Discontent breeds indulgent living, which often results in poverty. If you find yourself continually short on finances, make sure you are living within your means. Cultivate in your conversation with your children a continual thanksgiving for every provision of God. On the other hand, if you spend a lot of time pining through catalogues, talking about the things you desire, be sure this attitude will be observed by your children. We also need to continually remind our children that God has given us all that we *need*, and that He will always provide for us.

6. **Surety / countersigning on another's loan**

Here's just some down-to-earth practical advice: it is a bad idea to countersign on another's debt.

7. **Integrity**

It should go without saying that a Christian cannot use dishonest means to generate wealth. But how high a standard do we maintain for what is permissible? Several Scriptures mention the concept of "false balances." Scales were used in Old Testament times to measure the appropriate amount of a product being traded. (Some products—for example, bananas in most supermarkets—maintain the same standard of allocation in today's market.) Unscrupulous sellers (and buyers) could gain an advantage by using false weights to pervert the actual amount of product being traded. The buyer (or seller) would be deluded into thinking he is getting more than he actually is.

Carry this over to your life and consider how you sell or buy items, such as a house, car or anything else. Any deception—whether lying outright, exaggeration, withholding relevant information or employing psychological manipulation strategies—is sinfully using a false balance, regardless of the measurable success (pragmatism).

8. **Persuasion and marketing**

These principles are especially relevant to parents who own a business or have some influence in the business decisions at their place of employment, but all of us find ourselves needing to persuade others at some point.

There is a right means of persuasion: wisdom and sweetness of speech (Proverbs 16:21, 23). Cultivate these qualities. There are also wrong means of persuasion, including:

· Praising self (Proverbs 27:2)

· Showing partiality (Proverbs 28:21; James 2:1-9)

· Appealing to the flesh, such as sensuality or pride (Mark 9:42; 2 Peter 2:18)

· Putting others under compulsion (2 Corinthians 9:7)

The litmus test is Matthew 7:12, "treat people the same way you want them to treat you, for this is the Law and the Prophets" (NASB).

Paul, in Philippians 2:3, commands believers to "regard one another as more important than yourselves" (NASB). He goes on and does something absolutely amazing: he takes the incarnation, ministry and death of Christ—the pivotal events of all history—and does not teach any doctrine of Christ's substitutionary atonement, but uses them as an illustration of humility for us to follow. (!) The point is powerful: if Christ, out of obedience to the Father, voluntarily gave up His rightful privileges as God (while still remaining fully God) to take on human flesh and suffer humiliation and murder at the hands of unworthy sinners, how much more should we be willing to give up our "rights" and interests to serve others? Sadly, much marketing revolves around using others to satisfy our own interests, contrary to this command.

9. **Priorities: loving God or loving money**

As Paul says in 1 Timothy 6:10, "the love of money is a root of all sorts of evil" (NASB). Pursuing wealth causes us to neglect the more important things such as the Kingdom. And the pursuit of wealth has no finish line—we will never reach a point where we are satisfied. Setting our mind on Christ will cause us to see money as just another tool that can be used for His glory. Again, the things that make up our daily conversation with our family will impact the way our children develop their priorities.

Children need to be taught that money doesn't cause us to sin, but that lusting after money takes our eyes off God and leaves us prone to sin. We should keep our eyes on God and not on the things of this world. This type of teaching in the home can help children understand that they do not have to keep up with their friends who have the best computer games, etc.

10. Dependence on the Lord

We must never forget that it is the Lord who gives the power to gain wealth (Deuteronomy 8:17-18). Like the godless pagans who worship the creature rather than the Creator (Romans 1), prosperity can cause us to trust in the gift rather than the Giver. But "the uncertainty of riches" (1 Timothy 6:17-19, NASB) is an unworthy recipient of our trust (Proverbs 11:28, 18:11, 23:4-5; Luke 12:13-34). Remind yourself and your family continually that the money and things you enjoy today could be gone tomorrow and, if so, "blessed be the name of the Lord" (Job 1:21, NASB). Commit your ways to Him (Proverbs 16:1-3; James 4:13-16) and trust in His wisdom and direction.

11. Saving / Presumption

It is wise, the Proverbs say, to maintain savings for the future. Saving allows one to be available to the Spirit to meet a special need or an unexpected demand, or to provide an inheritance to the following generations. Saving is not a replacement for dependence on the Lord (Proverbs 18:11); it is presumption (Psalm 19:13; Matthew 4:5-7) to squander any margin with which He blesses you and expect Him to bail you out when a need arises.

12. Taxes

Our government, no matter how much we disagree with its decisions at times, has been instituted by God and is His servant (Romans 13:1-4), and we are commanded to pay our taxes faithfully (Romans 13:6-7). Just as in every other area, any form of deception or selfish manipulation to avoid taxes is sin.

Session 11: Getting Started

Allow participants to respond.

Session 11: Bringing It Home

1. Certain Jews felt they held special favor with God because they had a unique religious family heritage to cling to. "We are sons and daughters of Abraham," they boasted. But they misunderstood that it is not the family heritage that provides salvation. Salvation comes only through personal faith in our Savior Jesus Christ.

   We have the responsibility to tell others about the gospel.

The bad news is that the rebellion of the first man, Adam, against God's command brought death, suffering and separation from God into this world. We see the results all around us. All of Adam's descendants are sinful from conception (Psalm 51:5) and have themselves entered into this rebellion (sin). They therefore cannot live with a holy God, but are condemned to separation from God. The Bible says that "all have sinned, and come short of the glory of God" (Romans 3:23, KJV) and that all are therefore subject to "everlasting destruction from the presence of the Lord and from the glory of His power" (2 Thessalonians 1:9, NKJV).

But the good news is that God has done something about it. "For God so loved the world that He gave his only-begotten Son, that whoever believes in Him should not perish but have everlasting life" (John 3:16, NKJV).

Jesus Christ the Creator, though totally sinless, suffered, on behalf of mankind, the penalty of mankind's sin, which is death and separation from God. He did this to satisfy the righteous demands of the holiness and justice of God, His Father. Jesus was the perfect sacrifice; He died on a cross, but on the third day He rose again, conquering death, so that all who truly believe in Him, repent of their sin and trust in Him (rather than their own merit), are no longer separated from God and will live for eternity with their Creator.

Therefore: "He who believes in Him is not condemned; but he who does not believe is condemned already, because he has not believed in the name of the only-begotten Son of God" (John 3:18, NKJV).

What a wonderful Savior—and what a wonderful salvation in Christ our Creator!

2. Allow participants to respond.

3. Allow participants to share their responses—which could include books, television programs, movies, friends and extracurricular activities.

4. Allow participants to respond.

5. Allow participants to respond.

RESOURCES

- *The 7 C's of History* (*Answers in Genesis*)

- *A Christian Philosophy of Education* by Dr. Gordon Clark

- *A Faith to Grow On* by John MacArthur

- *Age of Opportunity* by Paul Tripp

- *Always Ready* by Greg Bahnsen

- *Answers Academy* (*Answers in Genesis*)

- *Beginnings* (*Answers in Genesis*)

- *The Christian and His Finances* audio tape by John MacArthur

- *Christian Living in the Home* by Jay Adams

- *The Complete Husband* by Lou Priolo

- *Does the Truth Matter Anymore?* DVD series by John MacArthur

- *"Don't Make Me Count to Three!"* by Ginger Plowman

- *Everyday Talk—Talking Freely and Naturally about God with Your Children* by John A. Younts

- *The Excellent Wife* by Martha Peace

- *Exegetical Fallacies* by D.A. Carson

- *The Exemplary Husband* by Stuart Scott

- *Fearfully and Wonderfully Made* (DVD)

- *The Forgotten Spurgeon* by Iain Murray

- *George Mueller of Bristol: His Life of Faith and Prayer* by A.T. Pierson

- *Heart of Anger* by Lou Priolo

- *How to Read the Bible for All Its Worth* by Gordon D. Fee and Douglas Stuart

- *Jonathan Edwards: A New Biography* by Iain Murray
- *John Bunyan: His Life, Times, and Work* by John Brown (available from Amazon.com)
- *Love Life for Every Married Couple* by Ed Wheat
- *Luther* (book or DVD)
- *Managers of Their Homes* by Steve and Teri Maxwell (available from Titus2.com)
- *Marriage To A Difficult Man: The Uncommon Union Of Jonathan And Sarah Edwards* by Elizabeth Dodds
- *Master Your Money* (book and workbook) by Ron Blue
- *Pilgrim's Progress* (book or curriculum)
- *The Revised and Expanded Answers Book* edited by Don Batten
- *Shepherding a Child's Heart* by Tedd Tripp
- *Spanking—A Loving Discipline* by Roy Lessin
- *Spurgeon: The Early Years*, Banner of Truth Trust
- *Spurgeon: The Full Harvest*, Banner of Truth Trust
- *Teach Them Diligently: How to use the Scriptures in Child Training* by Lou Priolo
- *War of the Worldviews* edited by Gary Vaterlaus
- *Wisdom for Today's Issues: A Topical Arrangement of the Proverbs* by Stephen Voorwinde
- *The Young Peacemaker* by Corlette Sande

These resources are available from
AnswersBookstore.com
or by calling 1-800-778-3390

INDEX